CAREER IDEAS

for kids who like

ART

DIANE LINDSEY REEVES

Illustrations by
NANCY BOND

Facts On File, Inc.

CAREER IDEAS FOR KIDS WHO LIKE ART

Facts On File, Inc.
132 West 31st Street
New York NY 10001

Library of Congress Cataloging-in-Publication Data
Reeves, Diane Lindsey, 1959–
    Art / Diane Lindsey Reeves.
        p.   cm.—(Career ideas for kids who like)
    Includes bibliographical references and index.
    Summary: Explores fifteen different career possibilities for
people who have artistic interests and aptitudes, including
animator, cosmetologist, chef, floral designer, interior designer,
and photojournalist.
    ISBN 0-8160-3681-0
    1. Arts—Vocational guidance—United States—Juvenile literature.
[1. Arts—Vocational guidance.   2. Vocational guidance.]   I. Title.
II. Series: Reeves, Diane Lindsey, 1959–   Career ideas for
kids who like.
NX503.R44   1998
700'.23'73—dc21   97-32687

Text and cover design by Smart Graphics
Illustrations by Nancy Bond

This book is dedicated to,
my nieces and nephews,
Ashley and Kyle Leafgren
and
Austin and Abbie Bryan.
You make it fun to be an aunt!

ACKNOWLEDGMENTS

A million thanks to the people who took the time to share
their career stories and provide photos for this book:

June Beckstead
Rebecca Black
Becky Borczon
Laurent Dufourg
Mary Engelbreit
Michael Graves
Anthony Grieder
Kaki Hockersmith
Judith Jamison
Barbara Luck
Rusty Mills
Gary Pettit
Michael Ritt
Stephen Shames
Richard Steckel

Also, special thanks to the design team of Smart Graphics,
Nancy Bond, and Cathy Rincon for bringing the
Career Ideas for Kids series to life with their creative talent.

Finally, much appreciation and admiration is due to
my editor, Nicole Bowen, whose vision and attention
to detail increased the quality of this project in
many wonderful ways.

CONTENTS

MAKE A CHOICE!

You're young. Most of your life is still ahead of you. How are you supposed to know what you want to be when you grow up?

You're right: 10, 11, 12, 13 is a bit young to know exactly what and where and how you're going to do whatever it is you're going to do as an adult. But, it's the perfect time to start making some important discoveries about who you are, what you like to do, and what you do best. It's the ideal time to start thinking about what you *want* to do.

Make a choice! If you get a head start now, you may avoid setbacks and mistakes later on.

When it comes to picking a career, you've basically got two choices.

CHOICE A

Wait until you're in college to start figuring out what you want to do. Even then you still may not decide what's up your alley, so you graduate and jump from job to job still searching for something you really like.

Hey, it could work. It might be fun. Lots of (probably most) people do it this way.

The problem is that if you pick Choice A, you may end up settling for second best. You may miss out on a meaningful education, satisfying work, and the rewards of a focused and well-planned career.

You have another choice to consider.

CHOICE B

Start now figuring out your options and thinking about the things that are most important in your life's work: Serving others? Staying true to your values? Making lots of money? Enjoying your work? Your young years are the perfect time to mess around with different career ideas without messing up your life.

Reading this book is a great idea for kids who choose B. It's a first step toward choosing a career that matches your skills, interests, and lifetime goals. It will help you make a plan for tailoring your junior and high school years to fit your career dreams. To borrow a jingle from the U.S. Army—using this book is a way to discover how to "be all that you can be."

Ready for the challenge of Choice B? If so, read the next section to find out how this book can help start you on your way.

HOW TO USE THIS BOOK

This isn't a book about interesting careers that other people have. It's a book about interesting careers that you can have.

Of course, it won't do you a bit of good to just read this book. To get the whole shebang, you're going to have to jump in with both feet, roll up your sleeves, put on your thinking cap—whatever it takes—to help you do these three things:

- ☼ **Discover** what you do best and enjoy the most. (This is the secret ingredient for finding work that's perfect for you.)

☀ **Explore** ways to match your interests and abilities with career ideas.

☀ **Experiment** with lots of different ideas until you find the ideal career. (It's like trying on all kinds of hats to see which ones fit!)

Use this book as a road map to some exciting career destinations. Here's what to expect in the chapters that follow.

GET IN GEAR!

First stop: self-discovery. These activities will help you uncover important clues about the special traits and abilities that make you *you*. When you are finished you will have developed a personal Skill Set that will help guide you to career ideas in the next chapter.

TAKE A TRIP!

Next stop: exploration. Cruise down the career idea highway and find out about a variety of career ideas that are especially appropriate for people who like art. Use the Skill Set chart at the beginning of each entry to match your own interests with those required for success on the job.

MAKE AN ARTISTIC DETOUR!

Here's your chance to explore up-and-coming opportunities in computer graphics and animation as well as the tried-and-true fields of fine arts, teaching, and basic design.

Just when you thought you'd seen it all, here come dozens of interesting art ideas to add to the career mix. Charge up your career search by learning all you can about some of these opportunities.

DON'T STOP NOW!

Third stop: experimentation. The library, the telephone, a computer, and a mentor—four keys to a successful career planning adventure. Use them well, and before long you'll be on the trail of some hot career ideas.

WHAT'S NEXT?

Make a plan! Chart your course (or at least the next stop) with these career planning road maps. Whether you're moving full steam ahead with a great idea or get slowed down at a yellow light of indecision, these road maps will keep you moving forward toward a great future.

Use a pencil—you're bound to make a detour or two along the way. But, hey, you've got to start somewhere.

HOORAY! YOU DID IT!

Some final rules of the road before sending you off to new adventures.

SOME FUTURE DESTINATIONS

This section lists a few career planning tools you'll want to know about.

You've got a lot of ground to cover in this phase of your career planning journey. Start your engines and get ready for an exciting adventure!

GET IN GEAR!

Career planning is a lifelong journey. There's usually more than one way to get where you're going, and there are often some interesting detours along the way. But, you have to start somewhere. So, rev up and find out all you can about you—one-of-a-kind, specially designed you. That's the first stop on what can be the most exciting trip of your life!

To get started, complete the two exercises described below.

WATCH FOR SIGNS ALONG THE WAY

Road signs help drivers figure out how to get where they want to go. They provide clues about direction, road conditions, and safety. Your career road signs will provide clues about who you are, what you like, and what you do best. These clues can help you decide where to look for the career ideas that are best for you.

Complete the following statements to make them true for you. There are no right or wrong answers. Jot down the response that describes you best. Your answers will provide important clues about career paths you should explore.

Please Note: If this book does not belong to you, write your responses on a separate sheet of paper.

7

On my last report card, I got the best grade in _____ .

On my last report card, I got the worst grade in _____ .

I am happiest when _____ .

Something I can do for hours without getting bored is _____ .

Something that bores me out of my mind is _____ .

My favorite class is _____ .

My least favorite class is _____ .

The one thing I'd like to accomplish with my life is _____ .

My favorite thing to do after school is _____ .

My least favorite thing to do after school is _____ .

Something I'm really good at is _____ .

Something that is really tough for me to do is _____ .

My favorite adult person is _____ because _____ .

When I grow up _____ .

The kinds of books I like to read are about _____ .

The kinds of videos I like to watch are about _____ .

GET SOME DIRECTION

It's easy to get lost when you don't have a good idea of where you want to go. This is especially true when you start thinking about what to do with the rest of your life. Unless you focus on where you want to go, you might get lost or even miss the exit. This second exercise will help you connect your own interests and abilities with a whole world of career opportunities.

Mark the activities that you enjoy doing or would enjoy doing if you had the chance. Be picky. Don't mark ideas that you wish you would do, mark only those that you would really do. For instance, if the idea of skydiving sounds appealing, but you'd never do it because you are terrified of heights, don't mark it.

Please Note: If this book does not belong to you, write your responses on a separate sheet of paper.

- ❏ 1. Rescue a cat stuck in a tree
- ❏ 2. Visit the pet store every time you go to the mall
- ❏ 3. Paint a mural on the cafeteria wall
- ❏ 4. Run for student council
- ❏ 5. Send e-mail to a "pen pal" in another state
- ❏ 6. Survey your classmates to find out what they do after school
- ❏ 7. Try out for the school play
- ❏ 8. Dissect a frog and identify the different organs
- ❏ 9. Play baseball, soccer, football, or _____ (fill in your favorite sport)

❑ 10. Talk on the phone to just about anyone who will talk back

❑ 11. Try foods from all over the world—Thailand, Poland, Japan, etc.

❑ 12. Write poems about things that are happening in your life

❑ 13. Create a really scary haunted house to take your friends through on Halloween

❑ 14. Recycle all your family's trash

❑ 15. Bake a cake and decorate it for your best friend's birthday

❑ 16. Sell enough advertisements for the school yearbook to win a trip to Walt Disney World

❑ 17. Simulate an imaginary flight through space on your computer screen

❑ 18. Build model airplanes, boats, doll houses, or anything from kits

❑ 19. Teach your friends a new dance routine

❑ 20. Watch the stars come out at night and see how many constellations you can find

❑ 21. Watch baseball, soccer, football, or _____ (fill in your favorite sport) on TV

❑ 22. Give a speech in front of the entire school

❑ 23. Plan the class field trip to Washington, D.C.

❑ 24. Read everything in sight, including the back of the cereal box

❑ 25. Figure out "who dunnit" in a mystery story

❑ 26. Take in stray or hurt animals

❑ 27. Make a poster announcing the school football game

❑ 28. Think up a new way to make the lunch line move faster and explain it to the cafeteria staff

❑ 29. Put together a multimedia show for a school assembly using music and lots of pictures and graphics

❑ 30. Invest your allowance in the stock market and keep track of how it does

❑ 31. Go to the ballet or opera every time you get the chance

❑ 32. Do experiments with a chemistry set

❑ 33. Keep score at your sister's Little League game

❏ 34. Use lots of funny voices when reading stories to children
❏ 35. Ride on airplanes, trains, boats—anything that moves
❏ 36. Interview the new exchange student for an article in the school newspaper
❏ 37. Build your own treehouse
❏ 38. Help clean up a waste site in your neighborhood
❏ 39. Visit an art museum and pick out your favorite painting
❏ 40. Play Monopoly® in an all-night championship challenge
❏ 41. Make a chart on the computer to show how much soda students buy from the school vending machines each week
❏ 42. Keep track of how much your team earns to buy new uniforms
❏ 43. Play an instrument in the school band or orchestra
❏ 44. Put together a 1,000-piece puzzle
❏ 45. Write stories about sports for the school newspaper
❏ 46. Listen to other people talk about their problems
❏ 47. Imagine yourself in exotic places
❏ 48. Hang around bookstores and libraries
❏ 49. Play harmless practical jokes on April Fools' Day

❏ 50. Join the 4-H club at your school
❏ 51. Take photographs at the school talent show
❏ 52. Make money by setting up your own business—paper route, lemonade stand, etc.
❏ 53. Create an imaginary city using a computer
❏ 54. Do 3-D puzzles
❏ 55. Keep track of the top 10 songs of the week
❏ 56. Train your dog to do tricks
❏ 57. Make play-by-play announcements at the school football game
❏ 58. Answer the phones during a telethon to raise money for orphans
❏ 59. Be an exchange student in another country
❏ 60. Write down all your secret thoughts and favorite sayings in a journal
❏ 61. Jump out of an airplane (with a parachute, of course)
❏ 62. Plant and grow a garden in your backyard (or on your windowsill)
❏ 63. Use a video camera to make your own movies
❏ 64. Get your friends together to help clean up your town after a hurricane
❏ 65. Spend your summer at a computer camp learning lots of new computer programs

❏ 66. Build bridges, skyscrapers, and other structures out of LEGO®s

❏ 67. Plan a concert in the park for little kids

❏ 68. Collect different kinds of rocks

❏ 69. Help plan a sports tournament

❏ 70. Be DJ for the school dance

❏ 71. Learn how to fly a plane or sail a boat

❏ 72. Write funny captions for pictures in the school yearbook

❏ 73. Scuba dive to search for buried treasure

❏ 74. Recognize and name several different breeds of cats, dogs, and other animals

❏ 75. Sketch pictures of your friends

❏ 76. Pick out neat stuff to sell at the school store

❏ 77. Answer your classmates' questions about how to use the computer

❏ 78. Draw a map showing how to get to your house from school

❏ 79. Make up new words to your favorite songs

❏ 80. Take a hike and name the different kinds of trees, birds, or flowers

❏ 81. Referee intramural basketball games

❏ 82. Join the school debate team

❏ 83. Make a poster with postcards from all the places you went on your summer vacation

❏ 84. Write down stories that your grandparents tell you about when they were young

CALCULATE THE CLUES

Now is your chance to add it all up. Each of the 12 boxes on these pages contains an interest area that is common to both your world and the world of work. Follow these directions to discover your personal Skill Set:

1. Find all of the numbers that you checked on pages 9–13 in the boxes below and X them. Work your way all the way through number 84.
2. Go back and count the Xs marked for each interest area. Write that number in the space that says "total."
3. Find the interest area with the highest total and put a number one in the "Rank" blank of that box. Repeat this process for the next two highest scoring areas. Rank the second highest as number two and the third highest as number three.
4. If you have more than three strong areas, choose the three that are most important and interesting to you.

Remember: If this book does not belong to you, write your responses on a separate sheet of paper.

ADVENTURE
❑ 1
❑ 13
❑ 25
❑ 37
❑ 49
❑ 61
❑ 73
Total: _____
Rank: _____

ANIMALS & NATURE
❑ 2
❑ 14
❑ 26
❑ 38
❑ 50
❑ 62
❑ 74
Total: _____
Rank: _____

ART
❑ 3
❑ 15
❑ 27
❑ 39
❑ 51
❑ 63
❑ 75
Total: _____
Rank: _____

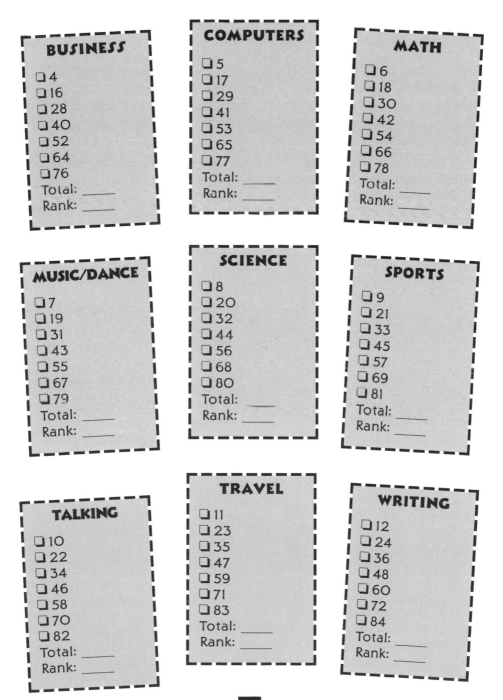

GET IN GEAR!

BUSINESS
- ❏ 4
- ❏ 16
- ❏ 28
- ❏ 40
- ❏ 52
- ❏ 64
- ❏ 76
- Total: _____
- Rank: _____

COMPUTERS
- ❏ 5
- ❏ 17
- ❏ 29
- ❏ 41
- ❏ 53
- ❏ 65
- ❏ 77
- Total: _____
- Rank: _____

MATH
- ❏ 6
- ❏ 18
- ❏ 30
- ❏ 42
- ❏ 54
- ❏ 66
- ❏ 78
- Total: _____
- Rank: _____

MUSIC/DANCE
- ❏ 7
- ❏ 19
- ❏ 31
- ❏ 43
- ❏ 55
- ❏ 67
- ❏ 79
- Total: _____
- Rank: _____

SCIENCE
- ❏ 8
- ❏ 20
- ❏ 32
- ❏ 44
- ❏ 56
- ❏ 68
- ❏ 80
- Total: _____
- Rank: _____

SPORTS
- ❏ 9
- ❏ 21
- ❏ 33
- ❏ 45
- ❏ 57
- ❏ 69
- ❏ 81
- Total: _____
- Rank: _____

TALKING
- ❏ 10
- ❏ 22
- ❏ 34
- ❏ 46
- ❏ 58
- ❏ 70
- ❏ 82
- Total: _____
- Rank: _____

TRAVEL
- ❏ 11
- ❏ 23
- ❏ 35
- ❏ 47
- ❏ 59
- ❏ 71
- ❏ 83
- Total: _____
- Rank: _____

WRITING
- ❏ 12
- ❏ 24
- ❏ 36
- ❏ 48
- ❏ 60
- ❏ 72
- ❏ 84
- Total: _____
- Rank: _____

What are your top three interest areas? List them here (or on a separate piece of paper).

1. _____

2. _____

3. _____

This is your personal Skill Set and provides important clues about the kinds of work you're most likely to enjoy. Remember it and look for career ideas with a skill set that matches yours most closely.

TAKE A TRIP!

Cruise down the
career idea highway
and enjoy in-depth pro-
files of some of the interesting options in this field. Keep in
mind all that you've discovered about yourself so far. Find the
careers that match your own Skill Set first. Then keep thinking
about the other ideas—exploration is the name of this game.

The following profiles introduce a variety of artistic careers.
You may be surprised to learn that there are so many options
that rely heavily on artistic ability and creative thinking.

Perhaps more than any other professional field, the artistic
field relies on show-and-tell—with an emphasis on show. Many
of these professions are visually oriented. As you read these
profiles, see if you can paint a mental picture of what each
career would involve.

Also, as you read about each career, imagine yourself doing the job, and ask yourself the following questions.

☼ Would I like it?
☼ Would I be good at it?
☼ Is it the stuff my career dreams are made of?

If so, make a quick exit to explore what it involves, try it out, check it out, and get acquainted!

Buckle up and enjoy the trip!

A NOTE ON WEBSITES

Internet sites tend to move around the Web a bit. If you have trouble finding a particular site, use an Internet browser to find a specific website or type of information.

Actor

SKILL SET

✔ **ADVENTURE**

✔ **ART**

✔ **TALKING**

GO take as many speech, voice, movement, and drama classes as you can.

READ biographies of some of your favorite stars.

TRY auditioning for school and community theater performances.

WHAT IS AN ACTOR?

Ready. Set. Action!

With those three words, actors assume new identities, go back or forward in time, and temporarily lose themselves in a fictional life in order to entertain, educate, or enlighten others. Good actors are so convincing that it's nearly impossible to separate the "real" people from the roles they've assumed.

Along with the ability to act convincingly, a great memory and thick skin are two other assets that actors must possess in great abundance. Actors must memorize entire scenes and recall countless genuine gestures and expressions. Above all, actors must be able to bounce back from the inevitable (and

often frequent) rejection that's part of this competitive profession. It takes a healthy dose of self-confidence and a deep commitment to acting to weather the ups and downs that are a normal part of life for all actors.

Acting is one of those "glamour" careers; it's so attractive that there are more starstruck actors than there are starring roles. That's why aspiring actors are often advised to "keep their day jobs." Maybe even more than with other careers, those who aspire to become actors must do so with their eyes open. And they need a good backup plan for earning a living while waiting for their "lucky break."

Keep in mind that Hollywood and Broadway aren't the only places to make a living as an actor. Other ways to satisfy the acting "itch" while keeping a roof over your head include performing in the following settings:

- community theater
- dinner theater clubs
- commercials
- educational videos
- theme-park productions

You might even want to consider teaching drama in a high school or coaching a children's theater program.

While it's true that only a few actors become superstars, it might just as well be you. So, hold tight to your dreams, make decisions carefully, and find creative ways to combine your interest in acting with making a living. Just remember, if you've got the acting bug—the show must go on!

TRY IT OUT

HOLLYWOOD, HERE I COME!

Drama camps for young people are located throughout the United States and in other parts of the world during the summer. You may also find a variety of after-school programs to choose from during the rest of the year. Any of these programs provides opportunities to learn the ropes in small productions, and they can be lots of fun. To find out about programs in your area, contact recreation centers, performing arts centers, and school drama teachers.

Two exceptionally good national programs that may be worth your consideration include

Missoula Children's Theater
(MCT, Inc.)
200 North Adams
Missoula, Montana 59802
406-728-1911

Up With People
1 International Court
Broomfield, Colorado 80021
303-460-7100

Once you have a little experience under your belt, you might want to consider getting involved in summer stock theater (summer camp programs for actors in which participants spend their time preparing for a special production). Programs of this type tend to be a bit more professional and are often an important early step in a budding career. To find out about nearby programs, request a directory from Theatre Directories, P.O. Box 5191, Dorset, Vermont 05251.

HELP WANTED

Scour the "audition" section in the classified advertisements of your local newspaper (the larger and more "artsy" the town, the more listings you'll find). Listings might include productions at colleges, community theaters, dinner theaters, and other centers. Look for roles that fit your age, gender, and experience level.

Find out all you can about the various roles and the audition requirements. Plan and practice an audition performance. Be prepared with an acting résumé and photographs of yourself. Take a chance and go for it!

If you aren't quite ready for the real thing yet, find out if the local library subscribes to trade magazines like *Billboard*, *Daily Variety*, or *Variety*. If so, look for a dream role and make a plan for getting it, although it will be a fictional plan at this point.

Think about the following questions: What image would you want to project? What would you wear? What type of scene would you prepare for the audition? Would you have to sing? Dance?

If the library doesn't have copies of these magazines, look for current copies of them at a larger bookstore or request review copies from

Billboard
Billboard Publications
1515 Broadway
New York, New York 10036

Daily Variety
1400 North Cahuenga Boulevard
Hollywood, California 90028

Variety
154 West 46th Street
New York, New York 10036

MIRROR, MIRROR ON THE WALL

Act out the following scenes (emotions, appropriate expressions, and all):

- getting caught in a lie
- sitting at the bedside of a friend dying
- reacting to winning the lottery jackpot
- proposing marriage to a reluctant partner
- greeting a long-lost sibling

At first, you may want to find a place where you can practice by yourself. Don't be trite or predictable in your responses. Try to be genuine, natural, and spontaneous.

Later, work up your nerve and get a group of friends together. Make a charades-style game of it with everyone taking turns acting out various scenarios.

Acting School for One

Video store here you come! Check out videos of Oscar-winning performances. One place to find a list of winners since the Academy's inception in 1927 is the *New York Public Library's Desk Reference*. It is available on-line or at your local library.

Carefully scrutinize the performances of old-time greats such as Bette Davis, Laurence Olivier, and Humphrey Bogart and recent winners such as Tom Hanks and Emma Thompson.

Take note of styles and the subtle nuances that make the difference between a good performance and a truly great one.

Compare the changes in acting techniques over the years. Learn all you can from the best. Don't forget that the key to your success will be developing your own personal style, not imitating someone else's.

BEHIND THE SCENES

It's not just *who* you know; it's also *what* you know that can make things happen for you as an actor. Learn all you can about acting and the behind-the-scenes aspects of the profession. A good place to start is with Cheryl Evans' and Lucy Smith's book *Acting and Theatre: An Osborne Introduction* (Tulsa, Okla.: EDC Publishing, 1995).

CHECK IT OUT

Actors' Equity Association
165 West 46th Street
New York, New York 10036

Actor's Fund of America
1501 Broadway, Suite 518
New York, New York 10036

Actor's Studio
423 West 44th Street
New York, New York 10036

American Alliance for Theater
and Education
Arizona State University
Theater Department
Tempe, Arizona 85287

American Association of
Community Theater
8209 North Costa Mesa Drive
Muncie, Indiana 47303

American Theater Arts for Youth
1429 Walnut Street
Philadelphia, Pennsylvania 19102

Associated Actors and Artists
of America
165 West 46th Street
New York, New York 10036

Performing Arts Resources
270 Lafayette Street, Suite 809
New York, New York 10012

Screen Actors Guild
7065 Hollywood Boulevard
Hollywood, California 90028

Show Business Association
1501 Broadway
New York, New York 10036

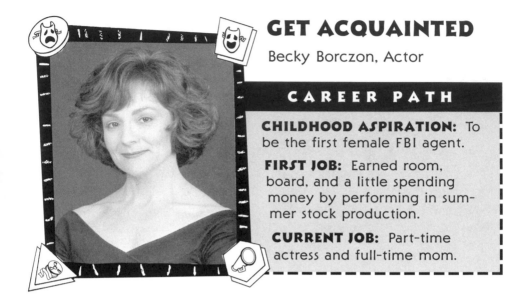

GET ACQUAINTED

Becky Borczon, Actor

CAREER PATH

CHILDHOOD ASPIRATION: To be the first female FBI agent.

FIRST JOB: Earned room, board, and a little spending money by performing in summer stock production.

CURRENT JOB: Part-time actress and full-time mom.

THE ACTING BUG BIT EARLY

From about as early as she can remember, Becky Borczon was starring in homegrown productions in her family's backyard or basement. Like Judy Garland in the old Andy Hardy movies, her rallying cry was "Hey gang, let's put on a show!" (If you don't know who Judy Garland was, ask someone over 40).

When she was in junior high, she learned from a favorite teacher that acting was something you could do for a living. By then she was hooked, and school productions and acting consumed all her free time.

LET'S MAKE A DEAL

When it came time to go to college, Borczon's parents were a little resistant to the idea of her pursuing a career as an actress. Wanting only her happiness, they were worried that the frequent rejection and sporadic earning potential might make for a hard life.

Together they came up with a compromise. They agreed to fund her education if she went to a liberal arts school first. So, she spent two years at Butler University in Indianapolis, learning about life and gaining a "big picture" perspective of the world.

When she continued to spend every spare moment in the university theater productions, her parents realized that acting wasn't just a passing fancy and gladly paid her way through three years of theater training at the Goodman School of Drama in Chicago. There Borczon was immersed in the world of theater 24 hours a day with classes in Shakespeare, voice, acting, and physical movement such as fencing.

She graduated with a degree, a well-rounded education, and a continuing passion for the stage. Her proud parents had the satisfaction of knowing that she was well prepared to make her way in the world.

THE LUCKY BREAK

After graduating, Borczon eventually made her way to New York in search of the bright lights of Broadway. She arrived with $200, a suitcase, and a generous friend with a spare couch to sleep on. It turns out that the friend's mother happened to work in the office of a prestigious acting company. She told Borczon about an opening in the cast. Borczon auditioned and got the job!

She spent the next couple years traveling around the country with this group, performing in classics such as those of William Shakespeare and Samuel Beckett. It was a great experience as an actor and a wonderful chance to see the country.

HAVE TALENT, WILL TRAVEL

Borczon's career has also included performing in regional theaters around the country. The downside of this experience was that it could get lonely working on the road. She'd be in one spot for a couple of weeks, head back to New York to line up another role, and then be off again. The upside was that in between performances she met her husband (then a dancer, now a doctor) in a karate dojo (school) where they were both learning martial arts.

Although rising television production costs are making opportunities rarer in New York, Borczon has also had the opportunity to appear on television. She recently completed two appearances on the program "Law and Order" and three on the soap opera "All My Children." Acting on location for television shows is especially fun, and Borczon enjoys the "perks"—trailers, makeup, and lots of free food! And the pay is good, too.

MAKING THE MOST OF THE DAY JOB

Like nearly every actor, Borczon has served time waiting tables. Although it wasn't exactly the stuff Emmy awards are made of, the experience provided plenty of opportunities for people-watching. Who knows? She might have been imitating your surly "Can't you see I'm starving here?" look in her last performance.

Fun as waiting tables may have been (note the sarcasm), Borczon soon realized that she'd be much happier if she were able to combine some of the best parts of acting with the continuing need for a regular paycheck. She found the perfect answer teaching aerobics to actors and dancers at a bodybuilding gym. There she found an enthusiastic audience, the opportunity to stay in shape, and a steady source of income to cover the rent.

Borczon says that she's noticed that actors who are able to make a satisfying connection between acting and earning a living are more likely to stick with the continual pursuit of the perfect role. The frustration level can get way too high when you're stuck in a job you hate while auditioning for acting parts.

STAY IN TOUCH

Here are two bits of advice Borczon would share with aspiring actors. First, be sure that acting is what you really want to do with your life. Take speech classes, be in as many plays as you can, and increase your chances for work by learning to sing, dance, and perform other skills. Also, take advantage of every opportunity to learn anything. Borczon has a friend who got a role because she was the only one at the audition who could drive a car with a stick shift. Sometimes these simple things can make the difference in winning the starring role.

Second, stay in touch with the real world. The temptation is great to just hang out with other people who want to act. Borczon says it's important to experience real life. Watch people and learn from how they walk, hurry to meet a plane, eat ice cream, and respond to everyday situations. Life itself is one of the best acting classes you'll ever take.

Animator

WHAT IS AN ANIMATOR?

Animation magazine's website says it best: "Animation has quickly become one of the most accessible artforms in the world today. From Mickey Mouse's *Steamboat Willie* to the most technologically advanced computer animation such as that used in *Toy Story*, the field has become a limitless icon of imagination for children and adults from all walks of life."

Whew! So you think using your artistic talents to make people laugh would be a fun way to make a living? Take this test to see if you could make it as a professional animator.

Pretend you've been hired by a studio to draw pictures for an animated cartoon show. As you're walking to your new workstation, the producer explains that in order to stay on schedule,

you'll need to draw cartoons for 10 to 20 feet of film each week. There are 16 drawings per foot of film. What happens when you multiply that? You'll need to produce 160 to 320 drawings each week. If that doesn't scare you off, keep reading.

Animation is a challenging, highly creative artistic endeavor. Quality and quantity count in this profession. Consider these tidbits about Disney's animated film *Beauty and the Beast.* The film

- contained 1,295 painted backgrounds
- included 120,000 drawings
- involved 370 people in its production (43 were animators)

Of course, computers help take much of the mindless repetition out of the task, but even the most powerful technology cannot replace creative imagination. Animators use it by the gallon!

Artistic talent is crucial, but it's just one of the required skills. Animators need to know as much about current events and human nature as they do about art and drawing. They need to understand how people think and why they do the things they do. They need to see the humor in everyday situations. Some cartoonists look at the dark humor or satire in important social issues.

Although there are no official education requirements for animators, it is obvious that the more you know, the more places you can go. Some animators choose trade school training in graphic design, while others pursue training in special art schools. Still others may opt for a liberal arts education at a four-year college. Experience, lots of practice, and a great portfolio are the keys to getting your foot in the door for a good job. The portfolio is especially important because it showcases your talent. A good one can be your ticket to your dream job.

Animators don't just work on movies. Newspapers, magazines, advertising firms, greeting card companies, and book publishers are other professional outlets for animators. New developments in multimedia, CD-ROM, computer games, and educational software are providing a wave of exciting opportunities for those with both artistic and computer skills.

Opportunity is out there. Work hard and prove that you've got the talent to make it on a professional level. Who knows? Maybe you'll become the next Walt Disney.

TRY IT OUT

SKETCHES TO GO

It goes without saying that if you want to be an animator, you need to learn how to draw cartoons. In fact, here is the first rule for any potential artist: Don't leave home without your sketchbook. Sketch scenes at school, objects lying around the house, nature images, and even other people. Create your own illustrations for a favorite book. Sketch along during your favorite television shows. You get the picture—draw anything and everything in sight.

If you aren't driving your family crazy with all your artwork, you aren't drawing enough!

ARTISTIC EXERCISES

You might be surprised at other techniques that some of the best animators use to hone their craft. Following are several ideas that will help you perfect your skills.

Take a dance class. Sure you can enjoy the exercise and all the great music, but as a potential animator you need an ulterior motive as well. Watch how the human body moves. Notice the angles and alignment. Even though your cartoon characters are likely to be caricatures of humans, they still need realistic human qualities that make them come alive.

Go to the zoo. Study the various animals and watch their reactions as they interact with other animals and people. What happens to a lion's mane when it roars? What about its tail and hind quarters? Be alert and teach yourself to notice the tiniest movements and reactions.

Be a people watcher. Airports are a people watcher's paradise. You'll catch an amazing array of emotions and reactions: the frantic traveler scurrying to catch his plane; the grandparents seeing their new grandchild for the first time; the tearful family saying good-bye to a son or daughter in military uniform. Make up stories to go along with each situation that you observe.

Get some culture. A great place to study human movement is at the ballet. Ask if you can sit in the balcony and sketch the dancers during their rehearsals.

Take a drama class. Animators are actors with a pencil. Learning how to act will teach you to understand how different characters would respond to different situations. It takes you out of yourself and into the lives and minds of strangers.

Tell a story. Volunteer to read stories to children at your local day care center or library. Animators tell stories with their drawings. Reading out loud gives you a feel for the structure and pacing of a good story.

TRICKS OF THE TRADE

As with any career, one of the best sources of information about animation comes from people who are already succeeding in the field. You have a special edge in animation because you can go to the local video store or library and borrow samples of some of the best work in the field. Easier yet, just tune into the cartoon station on your television.

Watch each program over and over again. Put things in slow motion and carefully observe the techniques and special touches that are effective. Stop the tape occasionally and sketch the scene. Take note of each character's position, the background scenery, and subtle differences between frames.

GET THE INSIDE SCOOP

Here's the not-so-secret code to finding out all about the field of animation: 778.5347. That's the classification number indicating the animation section at your local library. Go and look for books such as these.

Bendazzi, Giannalberto. *Cartoons: One Hundred Years of Cinema Animation*. Bloomington: Indiana University Press, 1995.

Culhane, Shamus. *Animation from Script to Screen*. New York: St. Martin's Press, 1990.

Glasbergen, Randy. *How to Be a Successful Cartoonist*. Cincinnati: F & W Publishing, 1996.

Taylor, Richard. *The Encyclopedia of Animation Techniques*. Woburn, Mass.: Butterworth-Heinemann, 1996.

Thomas, Bob. *Disney's Art of Animation: From Mickey Mouse to Beauty and the Beast*. New York: Hyperion, 1992.

While you are at the library, find out if they subscribe to *Animation* magazine. If you like it, consider saving up for a subscription of your own. This will keep you current on the latest technology, the best animators, and events in the industry. For subscription information, write to *Animation* Magazine, 5889 Kanan Road, Suite 317, Agoura Hills, California 91130.

CHECK IT OUT

For information about cartoonists, contact the following organizations.

American Council for the Arts
1 East 53rd Street
New York, New York 10022

American Institute of Graphic Arts
164 Fifth Avenue
New York, New York 10010

Cartoonist Guild
11 West 20th Street
New York, New York 10003

National Art Education
  Association
1916 Association Drive
Reston, Virginia 22091-1590

National Cartoonists Society
344 Brown Pelican Drive
Daytona Beach, Florida
  32119-1398

Contact the following places for information about some interesting specialties in this field.

Association of American Editorial Cartoonists
Ohio State University
242 West 18th Street
Columbus, Ohio 43210

Society of Children's Book Writers and Illustrators
22736 Vanowen Street, Suite 106
West Hills, California 91307

GET ACQUAINTED

Rusty Mills, Animator and
Television Producer

CAREER PATH

CHILDHOOD ASPIRATION: To be an artist.

FIRST JOB: Making drawings of toys for a major toy company.

CURRENT JOB: Supervising producer of animation at Warner Brothers Studio.

A childhood trip to the brand-new Walt Disney World decided Rusty Mills' future. He was so intrigued by the atmosphere that he wrote to the company as soon as he got home to find out how they did all that neat animation stuff. Much to his pleasure, someone wrote back and told him all about what it was like to be an animator.

Mills was also told that he would need a special camera to film his own cartoons. His father, who is also an artist, made a deal with Mills. If Mills painted the house, his dad would buy him the camera. The house got painted, Mills got his camera, and an exciting career was born.

A LITTLE LESSON LEARNED ALONG THE WAY

Never, ever send your own version of a popular cartoon character to its creator. Rusty learned this the hard way when he sent drawings of a famous duck to its famous creator. The duck's creator was not amused. He kindly suggested that Mills develop his own ideas.

The obvious lesson is that the person who created the character can always draw it better than you can. When you make contact with a professional, share your own characters. If you're good, they'll be impressed with your originality, and they'll appreciate your respect for their work.

HAVE YOU SEEN MILLS' WORK?

Mills obviously learned from that early mistake and went on to use his artistic talent in a variety of exciting ways. After a stint drawing pictures of toys for a major toy company, Mills went to Hollywood and started working for an animation production company.

Did you see the movie *An American Tail*? Remember the scene when Fievel and his father are talking about fish as they sail to America from Russia? Mills helped do the drawings for that scene. He currently produces the shows *Animaniacs* and *Pinky and the Brain* for Warner Brothers.

WELCOME TO THE REAL WORLD

The first day he got out of art school, Mills thought he'd have a job like the one he has now. Surprise! Fourteen years later, he's made it to where he wants to be. But like most professions, animation is a field in which you have to work your way up, prove yourself, and learn all you can about the process of making animated films.

BEHIND THE SCENES IN HOLLYWOOD

The pace is fast, and the schedule is everything. Mills has learned to discipline himself to get the job done—whether he feels like it or not. This particular trick of the trade is true for anyone who hopes to succeed in this environment.

Mills has learned something else while working with big name stars: They are all just regular people. This fact brings him back to earth when he starts taking himself too seriously. It also reminds him that anybody who's willing to do the hard work can be part of the seemingly glamorous world of Hollywood.

WHERE DO ALL THOSE WILD IDEAS COME FROM?

Coming up with a steady flow of creative story lines for shows like *Pinky and the Brain* and *Animaniacs* is a group effort. It starts with a staff of writers who meet regularly to discuss ideas. The eventual result of all their brainstorming is a script. At this point, the show's producers and directors jump in and make changes before accepting or rejecting the stories.

As supervising producer, Mills' job is to make sure that all the pieces fit. Whether it's the story itself, the background music, or the animation, he has to make sure that all the creative energy flows in the same direction.

NO EXCUSES

You don't have to starve to be an artist. There are plenty of ways to use artistic talent to make a good living. The opportunities are out there if you are willing to work hard and stick with it.

Architect

SHORTCUTS

GO collect pictures of interesting buildings. Keep these in a notebook and add comments about aspects you like and don't like about each structure.

READ about some of the different styles of architecture, for example, Gothic, Greek Revival, and Renaissance.

TRY building a structure with dry spagetti.

SKILL SET

✔ ART

✔ COMPUTERS

✔ MATH

WHAT IS AN ARCHITECT?

"Architecture is the imaginative blend of art and science in the design of environments for people." That's how the American Institute of Architects defines architecture.

Basically, what this means is that architects design buildings, homes, and other structures that people use for work, play, and everyday life. These include churches, hospitals, airports, indus-

trial complexes, and even entire communities. Architects use art and their creativity to dream up structures that are visually appealing. Everyone can appreciate a beautiful house or an imposing office building.

Looks are important but they aren't the only aspect of design that an architect must deal with. An architect must also make sure that the buildings he or she designs will actually stand up. This is where science comes into play. All those laws of physics and mathematics are applied in very important ways to make sure that structures can withstand the test of time. The architect's knowledge in math and science must be applied to details such as air-conditioning, heating and ventilating systems, electrical systems, and plumbing.

In addition, there are many legal issues to add to the equation. Architects must incorporate building codes, environmental concerns, fire regulations, and easy access for disabled people into the design process. They need to consider the wear and tear the building will be subject to by people using a structure day in and day out. And they must factor in an ample number of bathrooms and fire exits. They must also take precautions to insure a structure able to hold up to weather-related disasters, such as tornadoes and hurricanes.

With such a tall order to fill, architects need a fairly extensive education. The education process can be summed up in three steps. The first step is getting a five- to eight-year college education in architecture. College will include courses in art, engineering, history, and planning. The second step is to complete a paid internship with a certified architect that usually lasts three years. The final step is to complete a four-day exam to become a certified architect.

If you think you'd like to become an architect, make sure to take as many classes as you can in art and science. The American Association of Architects suggests that it's also important to cultivate an ability to see an object in space, a pattern, a method, a process, or a plan. Mathematical ability and drawing skills are definite pluses for the budding architect. It sounds rigorous, but it can be very rewarding if the idea of blending scientific laws with your own creative ideas appeals to you.

TRY IT OUT

TAKE A HIKE!

One of the easiest ways to learn about architecture is to look around. Open your eyes and start to notice all the details in the buildings in your neighborhood. Go for a walk downtown and jot notes (or sketch diagrams) about the buildings you find most interesting. What features make them notable?

Compare various schools, stores, churches, and other buildings that you frequent. Start looking for those details that give each structure an identity. Think about the how and why elements behind each aspect of the design. What would you have done differently if you had been the architect in charge?

ARCHITECTURE 101

What makes a Victorian home Victorian? What elements are always found in a Classical structure? The following activity will help you answer questions like this and will provide an introduction to some architectural basics.

Divide a notebook into sections allowing separate space for a variety of architectural styles. Make sure to include styles such as Victorian, Classical, Gothic, Roman, Greek Revival, and Renaissance. Find out all you can about each of these architectural styles (and others as you discover them). Write a description of all the elements that make each style unique. Include pictures or your drawings of identifying features. Whenever possible, include samples of famous buildings designed in each style.

A WINDOW IS A WINDOW IS A . . .

Good architects have to keep all their options open as they approach a new project. In order to do that, architects have to know what the options are. They must become experts in all the possible ways to achieve the same result.

Take windows, for example. Their purpose is basically the same in any structure—to provide light and ventilation. But, the difference between one garden window and two gabled windows can be striking. It's important to know the options!

Get out that notebook and pencil again. This time make a point of discovering all the different kinds of windows that you can find in your neighborhood and around town. Make a sketch of each style and learn its name. You may be amazed at the variety.

ON-LINE ARCHITECTURE
The Internet is a great source of information about architecture. Use your favortite search engine to find Virtual Library: Architecture. It's a virtual library for information related to architecture. Here you'll find information about current projects, famous architects, and links to other interesting websites.

RESOURCES FOR THE YOUNG ARCHITECT
For a chance to learn some fascinating facts about architecture and to have some fun testing your architectural skills, take a look at the following books.

Theriault, Florence. *This Old House*. Annapolis, Md.: Gold Horse Publishing, 1989.
Walker, Lester. *Housebuilding for Children*. New York: Overlook Press, 1990.
Wilson, Forrest. *What It Feels Like to Be a Building*. Washington, D.C.: Preservation Press, 1988.

If you can't find them at your local library or you'd like to obtain your own copy, these books and many other exceptionally good resources for students are available through the American Institute of Architects at 1735 New York Avenue NW, Washington, D.C. 20006-5292.

THE COMPUTERIZED ARCHITECT
Computers have dramatically changed the way architects do their jobs. If you'd like a chance to test your architectural

potential, perhaps you could invest in one of these computer programs:

ϒ 3D Home Architect, a CD by Broderbund, lets you create your own floor plans for remodeling a room or designing a whole house. You don't have to be an expert or an artist to use this. Contact your local software dealer or call 800-EGGHEAD to order a copy.
ϒ Microsoft's The Ultimate Frank Lloyd Wright introduces you to one of America's great architects and lets you tour some of his most famous structures. You also get tools to create your own architectural masterpieces. The ordering instructions are the same as above.

CHECK IT OUT

American Institute of Architects
1735 New York Avenue NW
Washington, D.C. 20006-5292

Association for Computer-Aided Design in Architecture
This international organization exists primarily through the Internet and considers itself a "virtual" organization. The address is http://www.acadia.org/

Association of Collegiate Schools of Architecture
1735 New York Avenue NW
Washington, D.C. 20006-5292

National Institute for Architectural Education
30 West 22nd Street
New York, New York 10010

Society for Architectural Historians
1232 Pine Street
Philadelphia, Pennsylvania 19107

GET ACQUAINTED

Michael Graves, Architect

CAREER PATH

CHILDHOOD ASPIRATION: To be an artist (ever since he was six years old).

FIRST JOB: Got his start in architecture working for a firm that specialized in designing consumer products as well as buildings in New York City.

CURRENT JOB: Architect, professor at Princeton University, and painter.

OFF TO A GOOD START

Even as a child, Michael Graves showed talent as an artist. As a young boy, he loved to draw. Lucky for him, his mother recognized his talent and helped him channel it into an artistic profession. She suspected that it would be hard to make a living as an artist, so she suggested architecture or engineering. Engineering was a bit too technical for Graves, so he set his sights on architecture.

ONE OF A KIND

The *New York Times* calls Graves "the most truly original voice that American architecture has produced in some time." That's quite a compliment, but it is not surprising: Graves is considered the "father" of postmodern architecture. (That means he was the first to apply these new concepts and is the best at it.)

His signature postmodern style consists of classical forms and natural materials. The result is an unmistakably unique blend of the traditional with the contemporary. His work tends to blend symmetry, well-organized space, and a touch of formality. He prefers warm, "livable" designs that are both traditional and uniquely innovative.

BOTTLE CAPS, TEAPOTS, AND BALLPARKS

From teapots and ballparks to bottle caps and Disney World hotels, Graves has lent his creative touch to a wide array of projects. His penchant for designing "things" as well as "places" began soon after graduating from Harvard University. The first firm he worked for specialized in consumer product design, in addition to building design. He developed an interest in this area, and to this day, it continues to be a major part of his design work.

A WORLDWIDE INFLUENCE

Belgium, Japan, Wales, Taiwan, and Germany are among the places where Graves' work stands abroad. Closer to home, you might want to take a look at some of these works of art.

- Denver Central Library in Denver, Colorado
- Bass Museum in Miami, Florida
- Clark County Library and Theatre in Las Vegas, Nevada
- University of Cincinnati, Science and Engineering Graduate Studies and Research Building in Cincinnati, Ohio
- Team Disney Building in Burbank, California
- Walt Disney World Swan Hotel and Dolphin Hotel in Lake Buena Vista, Florida
- Michael C. Carlos Museum of Art in Atlanta, Georgia
- Humana Building in Louisville, Kentucky
- Pace Theatre in Houston, Texas
- Texas Rangers Ballpark in Arlington, Texas
- Thomson Consumer Electronics Headquarters in Indianapolis, Indiana
- Whitney Museum of American Art in New York City

If you don't live anywhere near any of these places, you can get a sneak peek at a variety of Graves' works in his book of postcards entitled *Michael Graves Architect* (Rohnert Park, Calif.: Pomegranate Artbooks, 1994).

IF HE WERE YOUR AGE . . .

Graves says that one of the most important things that a young person considering a career in architecture can do is to get curious—about their surroundings, historic buildings, new structures, and other tangible evidences of modern life. He says that good architects will study the buildings of ancient Rome as well as the high-rises of modern Chicago. By seeing how buildings and styles have changed over time, architects see how our culture has changed.

He also recommends pursuing a well-rounded education—starting now. Take courses such as history, English, literature, art, and philosophy to become aware of political and social events as well as social trends. Becoming an avid reader of books, magazines, and newspapers is also crucial to learning how to understand how to build for people and the world in which they live.

HIT THE ROAD

Travel is another effective way to build awareness. For instance, an aspiring architect can compare the similarities and differences between Japanese and American houses by traveling through both countries. Graves recommends that architects visit different countries and regions as much as possible.

A FINAL WORD

Graves works from the premise that the past, the present, and the future are part of the same chain. By studying the past and present, an architect can design buildings that will be part of the future.

Artist

SKILL SET

✔ ART

✔ BUSINESS

✔ TALKING

WHAT IS AN ARTIST?

What's the first thing that comes to mind when you think about an "artist"? Does it involve someone painting scenes at the seashore while wearing a funny-looking hat and balancing a palette of paints? That's one of the many stereotypes often associated with the world of art.

The reality is that there are countless ways to make art the centerpiece of a rewarding career. An artist is someone who uses creative expression to produce works of art. The results of their work can exist simply for giving pleasure to others in mediums such as painting and sculpture. Or their work may serve both an aesthetic and a functional purpose. This means

43

that their work not only looks good but can be used. Examples are greeting cards, pottery, or some ceramics.

Whatever the artistic medium, whether it be watercolors or weaving, all artists must make a couple decisions in order to avoid another stereotype: the starving artist syndrome. An important goal of all careers is to make money, but for most artists, relying on their creative talent is not always sufficient to achieve this goal. That's where good business sense and strong communication skills can come in handy.

In order to make money, artists must find someone willing to pay for their work. Some artists do this through commercial methods, working for a company noted for producing and distributing various kinds of products. Others offer their work through art galleries, museums, and other retail shops. This method involves some legwork in order to find an ongoing source of space to show your work. Sometimes it takes an entrepreneurial twist to push an artist into the ranks of the comfortably self-sufficient.

This was certainly the case for one very talented painter. His work was good, but he just couldn't seem to sell enough of his works to stay afloat. He needed to do something else, but he knew that he'd never be happy doing something that didn't utilize his artistic skill. After thinking things over, he had a great idea. Instead of painting on canvas, he started painting on clothes—sweatshirts, jogging shorts, etc. He found some upscale boutiques to sell these items for him. When the orders started coming faster than he could paint them, he knew he was on to something.

The lesson here is that sometimes artists have to apply some of their creative energy to creating profitable avenues for their art. That element adds all kinds of interesting possibilities to the mix.

There really are no specific educational requirements for being an artist. It goes without saying that talent is the number-one prerequisite. Natural artistic ability is not something that can be taught—you either have it or you don't. The second most important prerequisite is building an exciting portfolio to showcase your experience and best efforts.

That second prerequisite makes many artists realize the need for advanced education. Even some of the most talented artists discover that pursuing a bachelor's or graduate degree in an area such as fine arts or art history adds a new, more developed and refined dimension to their artwork. Formal education is, of course, a must for those who want to teach or work in a museum.

Aspiring artists, take heart. Opportunities abound for those willing to work hard, perfect their craft, and look for creative ways to bridge the gap between starving artist and thriving artist.

TRY IT OUT

TAKE A CRASH COURSE IN ART HISTORY

Serious artists know who's who in the art world. You can learn a lot from other successful artists, especially those whose work has stood the test of time. Michelangelo, Leonardo da Vinci, and Vincent Van Gogh are just a few of the artists who continue to enjoy worldwide fame even centuries after they completed their works. Do yourself a favor and bone up on some of these great artists. Following are some suggested resources to make this task enjoyable and easy.

The beautifully illustrated Masters of Art series of books provides an interesting introduction to major eras in world history. It includes the following volumes.

Di Cagno, Gabriella, *Michelangelo*. New York: Peter Bedrick Books, 1996.
Loria, Stephano. *Picasso*. New York: Peter Bedrick Books, 1995.
Pescio, Claudio. *Rembrandt*. New York: Peter Bedrick Books, 1995.
Romei, Francesca. *Leonardo da Vinci*. New York: Peter Bedrick Books, 1994.
——. *Story of Sculpture*. New York: Peter Bedrick Books, 1994.
Salvi, Francesco. *The Impressionists*. New York: Peter Bedrick Books, 1994.

For another perspective on these and other artists, look for the Famous Artists series, published by Barron's Educational Series. This series provides an introduction to the life and work of other artists such as Paul Cézanne, Vincent Van Gogh, Claude Monet, Pablo Picasso, Henri Matisse, and Joan Miró. Facts On File's International Encyclopedia of Art series covers artists from around the world and includes information on women artists, Native Ameican artists, and folk artists.

Yet other interesting resources include the Art Activity Packs published by Chronicle Books. Each kit includes a full-color book about a specific artist and his or her work as well as stencil and poster activities for you to try. The series includes kits based on the work of Van Gogh, Pierre-Auguste Renoir, Monet, Matisse, Cézanne, and others. All are written by Mila Bouton.

For information about women artists contact the National Museum of Women in the Arts, 1250 New York Avenue NW, Washington, D.C. 20005-3920. Some books on women include

---

Berry, Michael. *Georgia O'Keeffe: Painter.* New York: Chelsea House, 1988.

Cruz, Barbara. *Frida Kahlo: Portrait of a Mexican Painter.* Springfield, N.J.: Enslow Publishers, 1996.

Plain, Nancy. *Mary Cassatt: The Life of an Artist.* Parsippany, N.J.: Silver Burdett, 1994.

Sills, Leslie. *Inspirations: Stories about Women Artists.* Morton Grove, Ill.: Albert Whitman & Co., 1989.

GO BACK IN TIME

Another useful resource to use in your quest for information about artistic greats is the Microsoft Art Gallery. This CD-ROM includes a collection of more than 2,000 masterpieces by art greats. Through the wonders of animation, you can actually witness each artist's technique and get a close-up look at their brushwork and use of color. It's like exploring the National Gallery in London from your own desk!

Look for this CD at your local software store or order it directly from Microsoft by calling 800-426-9400. Computer whizzes can order it directly on the Internet at http://www.microsoft.com. You'll need to have some means of payment at hand for either of these methods, so talk to your parents first.

KEEP A RUNNING LIST

Widen your artistic horizons by filling a notebook with all the different ways people make a living with their art. Start with some of the traditional methods such as painting, pottery, and weaving.

Keep your eyes open and add articles and descriptions of other creative outlets for artistic expression. For example, one artist in Arizona used the clay-colored dirt that is native to his region to color unusual T-shirts and other fashions. Another artist created Impressionist-style paintings of her clients' favorite photographs.

The possibilities are endless!

JUST DO IT!

Take advantage of every opportunity you can find to make art. Seek out opportunities to experiment with as many different mediums as you can. Use watercolors and pastels. Try clay and various textiles. Put mediums together in unusual ways. Doing this serves two purposes: You continue to perfect your skills, and you discover areas that make the most of your unique artistic talents.

Some of the ways to do this include taking art classes at school or through your community's continuing education program and signing up for classes in art studios or at art museums.

TELL THE REST OF THE STORY

Everyday life offers plenty of opportunities for creative expression. Take a sketchpad to the mall, airport, or park and find a comfortable spot to sit and observe. Watch as people interact with each other and with the environment. Sketch what you see in a series of scenes (something like a comic strip layout) and embellish each scene with your own ideas for the story behind the story. For instance, make up a story about the two people whom you saw emotionally embracing at the airport.

Another idea is actually to illustrate scenes from a favorite book of yours.

CHECK IT OUT

Allied Artists of America
15 Gramercy Park South
New York, New York 10003

American Art Therapy
  Association
1202 Allanson Road
Mundelien, Illinois 60060

American Crafts Council
72 Spring Street
New York, New York 10012

American Society of Artists
P.O. Box 1326
Palatine, Illinois 60078

National Art Education
  Association
1916 Association Drive
Reston, Virginia 22091

National Artists Equity
  Association
Box 28068, Central Station
Washington, D.C. 20038

National Association of Art
  and Design
11250 Roger Bacon Drive,
  Suite 21
Reston, Virginia 20190-5202

Sculptor's Guild
110 Greene Street
New York, New York 10012

GET ACQUAINTED

Mary Engelbreit, Artist

CAREER PATH

CHILDHOOD ASPIRATION: To illustrate children's books.

FIRST JOB: Working full-time at an art supply store.

CURRENT JOB: "Queen" of Mary Engelbreit, INK.

AUNT JEMIMA, BETTY CROCKER, AND MARY ENGELBREIT?

Not many people reach such a high level of success that their very name conjures up the image of a beloved product. For Aunt Jemima, it's pancakes and syrup. For Betty Crocker, it's cake mixes and cookbooks. For Mary Engelbreit, it's greeting cards, gift books, and hundreds of other charming products, all bearing her one-of-a-kind signature style.

The thing that makes Engelbreit different from the others is that she is a real person (sorry to break the news, but the other two are just marketing gimmicks). She is the creative force behind a company that has grown into a "mini-empire," with millions of avid collectors all over the world.

The people that know her best describe her as whimsical, nostalgic, playful, optimistic, and bit irreverent. That's exactly how her fans would describe her art, too!

IT DIDN'T HAPPEN OVERNIGHT

According to Engelbreit's mother, her daughter was drawing from the time she could pick up a pencil. By the time she was 11, Engelbreit had talked her mother into converting a linen closet into her very own art studio. She started out re-creating pictures from old storybooks (Johnny Gruelle's Raggedy Ann and Andy books were early favorites). She admits that she taught herself to draw by copying but says that if you copy something long enough, pretty soon you'll start drawing your own stuff just as well.

Later she began drawing pictures of scenes from favorite books such as *The Secret Garden, Jane Eyre, The Little Princess*, and the Nancy Drew series.

IN THE "YOU KNOW YOU'VE MADE IT BIG WHEN" CATEGORY

One of the artists that Engelbreit most admired was Joan Walsh Anglund. Anglund was among the first to introduce small, richly illustrated gift books filled with short, inspirational sayings. Even as a child, Engelbreit realized that this concept was something she could do as an artist. Now, some 30 years later, she is amazed (and very pleased) to find her own little books sitting on bookstore shelves right next to Anglund's. It marks one of those telling moments when desire and destiny intersect and make life come full circle. Maybe it sounds dramatic, but it happens to everyone at one point or another.

DON'T TELL ANYONE, BUT . . .

Even though Engelbreit had the potential to be an excellent student, she really didn't like school very much. By the time she made it through high school, she was ready to get out of school for good and get to work. In her mind, there was only one thing she wanted to do and that was to illustrate children's books. That she had no idea how to find paying work illustrating children's books was no deterrent.

Instead of college, Engelbreit embarked on a self-taught discovery of the world of art, and she credits several experiences for broadening her horizons. The first was her job at the art supply store. It was there that she discovered that there are many ways to make a living while making art. The next step was illustrating ads for a very small advertising agency. It was there that she learned about the business of art.

A transition into freelance illustration kept Engelbreit busy illustrating posters, ads, newspapers, and magazine editorials. However, she never lost sight of what she really wanted to do: illustrate children's books.

Later, her husband persuaded a friend in publishing to arrange some interviews with art directors. So Engelbreit put together a portfolio and took off for New York, certain that everyone would be eager to have her illustrate their books. But, much to her disappointment, no one jumped at the chance to put her to work. The last art director advised her to consider illustrating greeting cards.

A little insulted at first, it turns out that this advice became an important turning point in Engelbreit's career. That's because she took the advice and started producing greeting cards for other publishers. The cards were so successful that she started her own company and expanded her line to include other products.

In fact, it was her success in greeting cards that finally brought the opportunity to illustrate a children's book, an updated version of *The Snow Queen*, as well as a series of decorating, gardening, and crafts books and a whole line of gift books.

READ ALL ABOUT HER!

Chances are you can walk into any greeting card store in America and find samples of Engelbreit's work. Some find her work to be very addicting! Once you discover it, you might get hooked!

Another way to find out more about her work is to read the book *Mary Engelbreit: The Art and the Artist* (Kansas City, Mo.: Andrews and McMeel, 1996). It includes examples of her earliest drawings as well as those that have brought her the most acclaim. It also offers a lively description of her journey as an artist and businesswoman.

Also, she has available a special packet for aspiring artists. Send your request and a self-addressed, stamped envelope to Mary Engelbreit INK, 6900 Delmar, St. Louis, Missouri 63130.

Chef

SKILL SET

✔ ART

✔ MATH

✔ TALKING

WHAT IS A CHEF?

Chefs do not merely slap hamburgers on a grill. Chefs are artists who express their creativity with foods. Chefs are highly trained culinary artists who learn to make food look as good as it tastes. People pay top dollar to enjoy chefs' innovative and visually appealing dishes.

Chefs work in some of the finest restaurants in the world, as well as in corporate facilities, resorts, and other places where fine food is offered. Some chefs run their own catering companies and provide fancy menus at occasions such as weddings, sporting events, and black-tie affairs. For others, the ultimate symbol of success is owning their own restaurants.

Some of the better-known chefs publish their own cookbooks and host their own cooking shows on television. Others share selected trade secrets at upscale cooking classes or in magazine articles.

The work of chefs tends to be highly specialized with several kinds of chefs often presiding over specific areas of a busy restaurant kitchen. These specialties include

chef de froid, who designs and prepares decorated foods and artistic food arrangements for buffets in formal restaurants. This work can include making ice sculptures, molding butter into unusual designs, and decorating food trays using colorful fruits and vegetables.

executive chef, who takes charge of the total "back of the house," or kitchen operation. This chef supervises other chefs and manages the ordering and receiving of all food supplies. He or she also deals with management issues such as hiring, costs, quality, and product development.

pastry chef, who supervises and coordinates activities of cooks preparing pastries, desserts, ice cream, and other confections. This chef also makes pastry and table decorations using sugar paste and icings.

sous chef, who supervises and coordinates the activities of cooks who prepare, portion, and garnish foods. He or she may also cook and carve meats and prepare dishes such as sauces for special banquets or social functions.

To become a chef, you must earn at least an associate's degree in culinary arts. A good program covers topics such as American and international cuisines, nutrition, menu planning, customer relations, and some basic management issues. Any good program will also include extensive hands-on training in food preparation techniques. An internship experience, where you get the chance to put your newfound skills to work in the kitchen of a busy restaurant, is also an important part of the training process.

You may also want to consider pursuing a bachelor's degree in culinary arts management. The degree requires four years of training and provides more intensive training and preparation for the management side of things.

Since the experts project that jobs in food and hospitality industry are expected to increase by 42 percent by the year 2005, a good chef can expect a wide range of jobs from which to choose. If you have any doubts about that prediction, just look up all the restaurant listings in the yellow pages of any good-sized town, and you'll see that the possibilities for good chefs are nearly endless.

TRY IT OUT

WHAT'S FOR DINNER?

Your family's kitchen is a great place to test your desire to be a chef. Just step in and start cooking. Begin with the cookbooks you find there and cook foods that your family normally enjoys.

Branch out by checking different kinds of cookbooks out of the library and plan some interesting new menus. Make a list of the ingredients and ask if you can tag along on the next trip to the grocery store. Be sure to follow the directions carefully.

Make it a point to serve your meals with style. Use the nicest dishes (that your parents will allow), set the table, and maybe even add some candlelight and soft music. Remember that chefs have two goals when preparing food: making it taste good and making it look good. So, practice different presentation techniques and arrange the food nicely on each plate.

If you find that you reach the point where you'd rather be in the kitchen than watching TV and that you'd rather go grocery shopping than to the mall, you might be on to a great idea for your future occupation.

GET A JOB
The next best idea for you is to get a job in a good restaurant. Fast-food places provide certain job experiences, but the better restaurants are more likely to spark that connection between your artistic interests and a creative career path.

WATCH OUT, JULIA CHILD!
You may remember, when you were younger, the sheer joy of dumping miscellaneous ingredients into a mixing bowl and seeing what would happen. Now it's time to take a more mature approach.

A hallmark of great chefs is their unique recipes and creations. So start experimenting—a dash of this, a pinch of that. Who knows, you may come up with the next best thing to the hero sandwich.

READ ALL ABOUT IT
Magazine racks are full of tantalizing gourmet journals. These magazines profile up-and-coming chefs and restaurants, include yummy (and sometimes bizarre) recipes, and give a good overall introduction to the world of the food enthusiast. The next time you go to the grocery store or bookstore, flip through some of them and invest a few bucks in your career search.

WATCH THE GREAT ONES AT WORK
Julia Child, Craig Claiborne, and Paul Prudhomme are among the most well-known chefs in our country. Each has his or her own distinctive style and specialties. You can learn from master chefs like these three in two ways, without ever leaving home.

One way is to go to the library and look through the cookbook section. Check out any cookbooks or biographical materials on the chef of your choice. You may also want to ask the librarian to help you look up recent newspaper articles about them.

Another way to learn from famous chefs is to watch them on TV shows. Depending on where you live, you can find a number of gourmet cooking shows on TV. Most are aired during the day, so you may have to tape the shows on your VCR while you're at school. This is an entertaining way to watch the pros in action and to get some great recipes!

Make sure you keep some 3 x 5 index cards handy to jot down some of their tips and techniques. Label each card with the chef's name and include only one tip on each card. Stick with this for a while and in no time you'll have compiled your own reference of expert cooking techniques.

ON-LINE CHEF

There is a terrific website on the Internet called Online Chef. It includes interviews with famous chefs, menus, interesting new recipes, a glossary of food jargon, cooking tips and techniques, and all kinds of interesting articles. It's free and it's fun. Check it out at http://www.onlinechef.com.

HAIL TO THE CHEF!

Another interesting website belongs to the Club des Chefs des Chefs (loosely translated, Club of the Chefs to the Heads of State). This club is the exclusive domain of personal cooks to kings, princes, and presidents. The website gives us ordinary folk a chance to find out what it's like to work at such a prestigious level. Stop by at http://www.foodservice.ca/clubchef.htm.

CHECK IT OUT

For more information on opportunities for chefs, contact

American Culinary Federation
P.O. Box 3466
St. Augustine, Florida 32085

Council on Hotel, Restaurant and Institution Education
1200 17th Street NW
Washington, D.C. 20036-3097

National Restaurant Association
Educational Foundation
250 South Wacker Drive, Suite 1400
Chicago, Illinois 60606-5834

GET ACQUAINTED

Michael Ritt, Chef

Michael Ritt runs the kitchen responsible for serving 2,000–3,000 meals a day at a chain restaurant in Maryland. After starting out in his cousin's restaurant, Ritt spent four years earning culinary arts and restaurant management degrees from a prestigious culinary arts school. Since then, it's been a series of success stories for this talented chef.

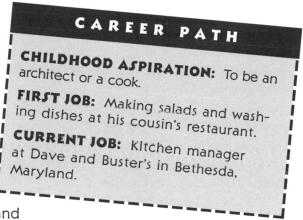

CAREER PATH

CHILDHOOD ASPIRATION: To be an architect or a cook.

FIRST JOB: Making salads and washing dishes at his cousin's restaurant.

CURRENT JOB: Kitchen manager at Dave and Buster's in Bethesda, Maryland.

THIS CHEF GETS AROUND

As with many professionals in the hospitality industry, chefs often have the opportunity to travel. Ritt has worked as an assistant kitchen manager on a kibbutz in Israel. He's also worked in various restaurants up and down the eastern U.S. coastline and specifically in the Hard Rock Cafe in Orlando and in Washington, D.C. In Paris he helped open a new American restaurant. Then he landed in the Big Apple with Planet Hollywood. From there he moved south a bit—to Dave and Buster's in Maryland.

BEST THING ABOUT BEING A CHEF

Ritt says it's fun to see people enjoying his food. And it's nice to know that since people always have to eat, a chef will always have a job.

WORST THING ABOUT BEING A CHEF

It's hard, physically demanding work, and the hours are notoriously long. Ritt typically works from 7:30 in the morning until

7:30 in the evening five to six days a week. He says that once you get used to it, it's not so bad, but it definitely keeps you hopping.

RITT'S SPECIALTIES

He makes a great seafood salad and loves experimenting with pasta dishes.

ADVICE TO FUTURE CHEFS

Find a mentor in the field—someone that you really look up to. For Ritt, they were his cousin and a college roommate. Both taught him a lot about the industry and set a standard for him to work toward. As he gained experience, he could look up to them and ask himself, "Am I good enough?"

Choreographer

SKILL SET

✔ ART

✔ MUSIC/ DANCE

✔ TALKING

GO dance, dance, dance!

READ about famous dancers and choreographers such as Fred Astaire, Martha Graham, Mikhail Baryshnikov, Agnes de Mille, and Tommy Tune.

TRY exploring your family's origins and culture through dance by linking up with the appropriate folk or ethnic dance group.

WHAT IS A CHOREOGRAPHER?

Dancing is where almost all choreographers get their start. It's not at all unusual for professional dancers to start learning their future profession when they are five or six years old. Most dancers have begun to show a serious interest (and the talent to match) by their early teens. That's not to say that it's impossible to get started any later; it's just unusual.

A dancer acquires self-discipline and physical stamina by faithfully adhering to a regimen of dance lessons and rehearsals throughout his or her young years. These attributes are absolutely essential for making it as a professional dancer. And, making it as a professional dancer is the standard prerequisite for becoming a choreographer.

Since one of the main functions of a choreographer's job is to invent dances, it makes sense that a choreographer needs plenty of dance experience to do that. The old adage—"those who can do, those who can't teach"—does not apply here. Choreographers have to know their stuff and be able to dance it too!

Choreographers are dance makers. They create patterns of movement and arrange steps or sequences of movement in such a way that they tell a story, make a statement, or express an emotion. As inventors of new and exciting forms of movement, they are always looking for unusual ways to

put movement, steps, and music together.
Quite often the choreographer must act like a
matchmaker, arranging a perfect marriage
between a musical composition and its interpretation in dance.
In simplest terms, a choreographer's job consists of three
parts:

☀ creating steps and movement to fit a particular purpose
or musical selection
☀ teaching dancers how to perform the piece
☀ directing dancers during performances

Other, less obvious, requirements for the job include having
excellent people and motivational skills. Knowing how to work
well with people comes in very handy when dealing with the
temperamental types who find their way into a production. The
motivational skills are invaluable for encouraging top-notch
performances out of dancers who have been touring for weeks
and are running out of steam.
Dance itself is the most important training requirement for
choreographers. Many colleges and universities offer excellent
preparation for this profession through their physical education,
music, theater, or fine arts departments. A well-rounded program will provide experience in music, theater, costuming,

camera and editing techniques, and other aspects of creative art. Many programs also offer opportunities to gain experience in actually staging and participating in productions.

There are some that would argue that a formal education can be a detriment to a career in dance because it requires too much time away from actually performing. In fact, a study of choreographers conducted by the National Endowment for the Arts discovered that although choreographers as a whole tended to be well educated, the average income reported for respondents with college degrees was far lower than the average income for those respondents without college degrees. That's not to say that education isn't important. It's just that talent and drive may be even stronger factors in determining one's success in this challenging profession.

Choosing the best education and training is something that is worth serious consideration by anyone pursuing a career in dance. Whatever route you take, count on dance lessons, rehearsals, and lots of daily practice being a big part of your life. Martha Graham, one of America's most admired choreographers, defined dance as "the hidden language of the soul." To find out if dance is a part of your destiny, listen and see if it whispers your name.

TRY IT OUT

FRIDAY NIGHT AT THE MOVIES

Dancers work in musical theater, film, and video, as well as in the ballet and concert field. You'll want to learn as much as you can about each of these forums for dance. Fortunately, there's a simple way to do this: Watch dancers dance. Go to concerts, watch the old musicals, see the newest moves in the latest music videos.

Make sure to observe films from every era: Start with some of the classics, starring Fred Astaire and Ginger Rogers, bop into the 1950s with *Grease*, and go disco-crazy with *Saturday Night Fever*. Pay special attention to how the dance scenes are choreographed. Feel free to dance along!

MAKE THE RIGHT MOVES

If you are absolutely new to the world of dance, you'll want to start with the basics. To get an insider's perspective on dance positions, performance techniques, and various forms of dance, check out *The Young Dancer* by Darcy Bussell, with Patricia Linton (New York: DK Publishing, 1994).

SHARE YOUR TALENT

Underneath all the glamour and hard work, choreography eventually boils down to one thing: teaching other dancers. Successful choreographers ensure that the dancers understand not only the movements but also the mood and perspective behind each dance. This advanced teaching skill is acquired only through lots of practice and fully developed communication skills.

If you've been studying dance for a number of years, you may be ready to start sharing your skill with others. Talk to your dance instructors about helping teach classes for younger or less advanced students. Pour your heart into it, and you'll be rewarded every time one of your young protégés performs on stage.

DANCE MAKERS

Choreographers are professional dance makers. If you have access to a cassette or CD player and know some good moves, you have everything you need to become an amateur choreographer. Pick a favorite piece of music and invent a dance that expresses what you feel when you listen to it. Work on it. Revise and perfect. Keep going until you feel completely immersed in the music and movement. When you are ready, perform your dance for your family or a group of friends.

When you really think you're ready, enter a choreographic competition. *Dance Magazine* lists all kinds of opportunities such as competitions and auditions. Each issue also contains profiles, news, reviews of performances, information on books and other resources, schools, health, and techniques. If you're serious about dance, subscribing could be a worthwhile investment. For information, contact *Dance Magazine*, 33 West 60th Street, New York, New York 10023.

DANCING IN CYBERSPACE

Following are a few exceptional Internet websites you can visit to learn more about choreography and other aspects of dance.

- The San Francisco Ballet at http://www.sfballet.org
- BalletWeb index at http://www.novia.net/~jlw/ index. html
- Behind-the-scenes stories from leading stage man-agers and choreographers at http://www.aahperd.org, which links to the National Dance Association and other fun sites.
- The Carnegie Mellon Center for Art Management and Technology at http://www.artsnet.org/Artsites/Dance. html

DANCING FOR A LIVING

The National Dance Association publishes a booklet called *Dance: A Career for You.* It describes various career opportu-nities for dancers including teacher, therapist, recreation leader, and, of course, choreographer. Request a copy from the address listed in the Check It Out section.

Once you've had a chance to read it over, make a chart list-ing each of the options with space to write down a comparison of the pros and cons of each.

CHECK IT OUT

American Dance Guild
31 West 21st Street, Third Floor
New York, New York 10010

Choreographers Guild
256 South Robertson
Beverly Hills, California 90211

Choreographers Theatre
94 Chambers Street
New York, New York 10007

Dance Notation Bureau
31 West 21st Street, Third Floor
New York, New York 10010

Dance Theatre Workshop
219 West 19th Street
New York, New York 10011

Dance/USA
777 14th Street NW, Suite 540
Washington, D.C. 20005

National Dance Association
1900 Association Drive
Reston, Virginia 22091-1502

Professional Dance Teachers Association
P.O. Box 91
Waldwick, New Jersey 07463

Society of Stage Directors and Choreographers
1501 Broadway
New York, New York 10036

GET ACQUAINTED

Judith Jamison, Choreographer, Dancer, Artistic Director

CAREER PATH

CHILDHOOD ASPIRATION: To be a dancer.

FIRST JOB: Teaching dance.

CURRENT JOB: Artistic director at the Alvin Ailey American Dance Theater.

BORN TO DANCE

According to her mother, Judith Jamison had a dancer's long legs and slender fingers even as a baby. She was so active that she wore out a couple of cribs by jumping around in them constantly.

Fortunately, she never outgrew all that energy, and her wise mother helped her channel it into dancing when Jamison was just six years old. Dancing has been a major part of Jamison's life ever since. By age eight she was dancing on pointe and says that the shoes "felt like iron booties." At age 10, her teacher often used her to demonstrate proper dance combinations to classes full of adults. By the time she was 14, Jamison was teaching younger children with a focused determination that was well beyond her years.

BREAKING THE BARRIERS
Most dancers are female, petite, and white. Jamison *is* a woman, but she's a very tall, African-American woman. As with anyone who goes against the status quo, she's had to work hard to prove herself and forge her own unique identity.

COLLISION WITH DESTINY
While Jamison was still a student at the Philadelphia Dance Academy, she went with some classmates to see a performance of the Alvin Ailey American Dance Theater. Watching the performance of *Revelations*, and inspired by one dancer in particular, Jamison was struck by the realization that "I can do that." Little did she know how closely her future would be linked with this famous dance company.

THE LUCKY BREAK
It was eight o'clock at night. Jamison had already taken five classes, and she was exhausted. Agnes de Mille (a legend in American dance) was on campus to teach a master class. (In a master class, someone who is especially good and well known teach advanced students.) As much as she admired Agnes de Mille, the last thing Jamison wanted to do was take another class. Some friends talked her into it. It's a good thing. That was the night Jamison was "discovered."

De Mille immediately recognized Jamison's exceptional talent. She invited her to come to New York to be in a new ballet called *Four Marys* that she was choreographing for the American Ballet Theatre. Needless to say, Jamison said yes.

COLLISION WITH DESTINY, PART II
Ironically, Jamison ran into Alvin Ailey after completely bombing out during an audition. In tears, she was so upset that she

barely saw him. But, he had seen her—and the raw potential in her performance. He called her three days later to invite her to join his dance company. She became a member of the Alvin Ailey American Dance Theater in 1965. She toured the United States, Europe, Asia, South America, and Africa, danced with many of the world's greatest male dancers, and delighted audiences everywhere throughout the 15 years she danced with the company.

All this the result of chance encounter in a hallway? Jamison prefers to think it was more like divine guidance. Those that have seen her dance would definitely agree.

BE READY WHEN SUCCESS COMES KNOCKING

In her autobiography, *Dancing Spirit* (New York: Doubleday, 1993), Jamison says:

> A lot of young people I meet do not know what they want to do with the rest of their lives, while it's getting later and they're under pressure to make a decision. It's for them not to worry, but to be well prepared, open, and educated. Learn as much as you can about everything. It's hard to tell young people to be patient, but that's what they need to be.

P.S.

Speaking of Jamison's autobiography, get it, read it, enjoy it, and learn some valuable lessons from someone who's made an incredible contribution to the world of dance.

Cosmetologist

WHAT IS A COSMETOLOGIST?

Cosmetologists work with individuals of all ages to keep them looking good. They routinely perform hair care procedures such as shampooing, styling, coloring, perming, and straightening. They can be most creative when they determine how to enhance each person's appearance with just the right style. Such creativity involves breaking out of a "cut of the month" mode and instead adapting the latest hairstyle trends into unique and attractive styles.

While hairstylist may be the first specialty that comes to mind, there are actually a number of additional specialties associated with cosmetology.

Estheticians specialize in skin care, body care, and makeup. While many work in beauty salons or spas, others work as makeup artists for television and movie studios or with plastic surgeons and dermatologists.

Electrologists specialize in removing unwanted hair from various parts of the body.

Manicurists specialize in hand and nail care. Manicures and pedicures are traditional services. As more women have discovered the convenience and appeal of various types of artificial nails, many salons and boutiques specialize exclusively in nail care.

Other possibilities include working as a photo stylist, a representative for a cosmetic company, a fashion consultant, or a cosmetology school instructor.

Cosmetology can also be an appealing option for those interested in owning their own businesses. In fact, owning or managing a salon is frequently part of the career progression for a successful cosmetologist.

In the United States, cosmetologists must become licensed before beginning to serve the public. Depending on the state, you can expect to spend between 1,000 hours (6 months) to 2,500 hours (15 months) in training. Cosmetology training includes classroom instruction in subjects such as hygiene and business practices as well as training in specific services such as facials and hair and scalp treatment. A good portion of the training involves practicing and actually performing the techniques learned in class.

Cosmetology training is often offered through high school vocational and technical training programs. You'll want to find out if this is an option in your school. However, before enrolling in any cosmetology training program, make sure that it has a good reputation. The early training you receive can make a big difference in determining who wants to hire you when you get out. Get the best, most reputable training you can find.

Actually obtaining a license involves providing proof of training, passing a written exam, and demonstrating various cosmetology services such as cutting, perming, and styling someone's hair. Before you even start thinking about licensing exams, you'll want to make sure that you pass these four tests.

- ✦ Attitude check. Are you friendly? Do you enjoy working with people? How well do you handle criticism?
- ✦ Artistic aptitude. Are you creative? Do you like to experiment with different styles and fashions? Are you willing to try new things?
- ✦ Care quotient. All aspects of cosmetology involve serving people in a very personal way. Do you care enough about people to do your very best work day after day, client after client? Is it important to you to boost others' self-esteem by improving their appearance?
- ✦ Physical fitness. Are you in good health? Do you have the stamina to work on your feet every day in a physically demanding profession?

In the United States, beauty salons serve at least 2 million people every day. That means there are plenty of employment opportunities for those with talent and perseverance.

TRY IT OUT

BEFORE AND AFTER

Get a group of friends together who share an interest in fashion and style. Ask each person to style their hair and to dress in their usual way. Take a "before" picture of each individual.

Experiment with new makeup, clothes, and hairstyles (no cutting, please). When you're satisfied with the new look, take an "after" picture of each person. Take the film to a one-hour photo developing company and enjoy seeing the results of your efforts.

For inspiration before you attempt the makeovers, take a look at the following book:

Kibbe, David, *David Kibbe's Metamorphosis*. New York: Atheneum, 1987.

Also, "before and after" stories are often a feature in many fashion and women's magazines such as *Family Circle, McCall's,* and *Good Housekeeping.* Thumb through past issues at the library to get more ideas.

BEAUTY BY THE BOOK
Start keeping a scrapbook of hairstyle and makeup ideas. You'll find tons of this kind of information (with some great photographs) in any fashion magazine. Clip pictures and add your own notes.

CUT OR DARE
Whatever you do, *don't* start experimenting with scissors on your hair or anyone else's. Instead, fine-tune your technique on hair that is not attached to a human head. Garage sales and thrift stores can be inexpensive sources of wigs. Feel free to practice styling and cutting to your heart's content without worrying about making mistakes.

LATHER UP
If you think you might like to become a cosmetologist but aren't sure, spend some time hanging out at a few good salons. You might even arrange to help out by shampooing clients or cleaning up for a favorite stylist in exchange for watching them work their beauty magic.

VIRTUAL BEAUTY
You can learn a lot about this profession without leaving home by tapping into Internet resources. First stop is the Beauty Net at http://www.beautynet.com. Here you'll find a virtual hair studio, skin-care suite, makeup counter, tanning room, and nail bed. You'll also find out about new products and the latest trends.

Another fun stop is the Beauty Tech at http://www.beautytech.com. This site offers links to beauty industry sites and nformation about hair and nails.

CHECK IT OUT

American Beauty Association
401 North Michigan Avenue
Chicago, Illinois, 60611-4206

Canadian Cosmetics Careers
Association, Inc.
26 Ferrah Street
Unionville, Ontario L3R 1N5

Hair International
P.O. Box 273
Palmyra, Pennsylvania 17078-0273

National Association of
Accredited Cosmetology Schools
5201 Leesburg Pike, Suite 205
Falls Church, Virginia 22041

National Beauty Career Center
3 Columbia Circle Drive
Albany, New York 12212

National Cosmetology Association
3510 Olive Street
St. Louis, Missouri 63103

GET ACQUAINTED

Laurent Dufourg, Hairstylist

CAREER PATH

CHILDHOOD ASPIRATION: To become a musician.

FIRST JOB: Shampoo boy at a salon in France.

CURRENT JOB: Owner of Privé, an upscale beauty salon favored by many Hollywood celebrities.

MARCHING TO A DIFFERENT DRUM

Whenever she couldn't find a baby-sitter, Laurent Dufourg's mother took her son to the beauty salon on Saturdays. Now known on a professional basis simply as Laurent, he has fond childhood memories of days spent hanging out and trying to help by sweeping the floors while his mother tended to her hair and beauty regimen.

When it came time to pursue a career, however, his first choice was to become a musician. As a teen growing up in Biarritz, France, he played in a band and had big hopes for a music career. When he was 16 and needed money to buy new drums, his friend found him a summer job as a shampoo boy at a local hair salon.

Laurent discovered that he really liked the creative aspect of styling and knew this was the type of work he could enjoy. So, he arranged to apprentice with the world famous Claude Maxime in Paris and spent three years working and learning in the salon's various departments. (France doesn't require beauty school licensing like the United States does. Instead, stylists are trained through apprenticeships with established salons.)

A few years later, a client asked him to go to Spain as her personal stylist. This assignment took him to a beautiful resort on the Costa del Sol. Discovering a serious lack of beauty care services there, he opened two salons of his own. Both were a big hit with the wealthy and famous people who frequented the resort.

When his family relocated to Los Angeles, Laurent became partners with the famous hairstylist Jose Eber. They opened and operated five highly successful salons. In 1995, Laurent sold his share in this business to open Privé, his own salon on Melrose Place. The business has expanded to include branches in New York and Las Vegas and an exclusive line of hair-care products called Laurent D.

ALL IN A DAY'S WORK

On any given day, Laurent might be booked solid with appointments with glamorous stars such as Gwyneth Paltrow, Sharon Stone, Alicia Silverstone, or Lisa Kudrow. Or he might fly out to London for the day to do Uma Thurman's hair for a photo shoot. Another day might find him busy meeting with movie producers, directors, the wardrobe consultant, and makeup artists to discuss just the right look for Elisabeth Shue's new movie. A hard day's work might be capped off by escorting a client such as Paula Abdul to a movie premiere or award ceremony.

Not all jobs in cosmetology are this glamorous, but it's not hard to believe that Dufourg really loves his work. He says it's fun to be part of all the excitement in Hollywood.

WHEN LESS IS MORE

Two traits have helped Dufourg earn his reputation as a world-class hairstylist. First, Dufourg's clients know that they can trust him to be diplomatic and discreet. His elegant European sense of style and his genuine concern for his clients serve him well in a profession so reliant on forming good relationships with people.

Second, it is Dufourg's trademark to cut and style hair in ways that perfectly fit each client's looks, personality, and lifestyle. His goal is to keep things as simple as possible because he understands that people are far too busy to have complicated hairstyles.

Together, these traits combine to keep an impressive list of clients happy and coming back for more.

THE SECRET TO HIS SUCCESS

Dufourg says a stylist can never stop learning. He keeps up with the latest trends and techniques by attending fashion shows and special training classes, reading magazines, and always being on the lookout for good ideas he can reinvent for a particular client.

Development Director

SHORTCUTS

GO do some extra chores and donate your earnings to a nonprofit organization whose work you admire.

READ about some traditional philanthropists of America's past—the Roosevelts, Rockefellers, and Vanderbilts—as well as those of today— Bill Gates of Microsoft, J. Paul Getty Jr., heir to the Getty oil fortune, and Joan Kroc, widow of Ray Kroc, founder of McDonald's.

TRY watching a fund-raising telethon on TV (Jerry Lewis' annual Labor Day telethon has become an American tradition).

WHAT IS A DEVELOPMENT DIRECTOR?

Development directors, or fund-raisers, find creative ways to raise money for charitable causes. If the arts is your passion but not necessarily your forte (for example, you love ballet, but you can't dance), a career in development can put you right in the thick of things.

The best fund-raisers raise money for charitable causes that they really believe in. It's a lot easier to ask someone for money if you believe that it changes lives or somehow makes the world a better place.

Most fund-raising is quite sophisticated. Successful fund-raising usually involves researching likely sources of support (wealthy individuals, foundations, corporations, etc.), writing compelling grant proposals, organizing appealing programs, and maintaining long-term relationships with potential donors.

Most fund-raisers are employed by a specific organization—a performing arts group, museum, or social service program. Some fund-raisers specialize in planning special events such as charity balls, telethons, or walkathons. Others work for consulting firms that specialize in managing major fund-raising campaigns for projects such as building a multimillion dollar performing arts center.

You can also work for an organization that makes donations. Foundations and many large corporations actually employ people to give money away to carefully selected worthy causes. At foundations these people are usually called grant officers or administrators, and at corporations they are usually part of the public relations or community development staff.

Helping the arts (or another cause) flourish, giving away someone else's money—these are some careers to consider if you enjoy "doing good." What a way to make a living!

TRY IT OUT

JOIN THE CLUB!

Arts organizations everywhere would welcome your interest in volunteering. Even though you don't get paid, carefully chosen volunteer projects will give you two important benefits. First, you get a chance to lend a hand to a cause you believe in or enjoy. Second, it gives you experience and contacts for future reference.

Be prepared: most volunteering involves varying degrees of behind-the-scenes dirty work. Play it smart; give every task your best effort. Such sacrifices have a way of paying big dividends down the road.

JUST DO IT!

You've probably been fund-raising since you were in kindergarten but didn't realize it. All those candy sales, car washes, and silent auctions are ways that schools, clubs, churches, and other groups make money for special projects (such as buying computers, playground equipment, and band uniforms). Get some more practice as a fund-raiser for your school. Hustle, think up new ways to sell; it's all for a great cause. Always remember these rules of thumb, however: Get your parents' permission, let them know where you'll be and for how long, stick around familiar territory, and always move around in groups—never work alone.

THE MILLION-DOLLAR QUESTION: WHAT WORKS?

Add up all the fund-raisers that a typical school sponsors each year—with sports teams, clubs, the band, etc.—and you're likely to have the makings of some great market research.

First, ask around and find out what groups did to earn money. Second, make a chart. Put the name of the group in one column, the type of fund-raiser in another, and the purpose of the fund-raiser in another. Next, ask the person in charge of the group for details about how much they earned. Get as specific as possible. For instance, ask how many items were sold, at what cost, and for what profit. Also find out how many people helped and, if possible, find out about how much time each person spent on the project. Add this information to your chart.

Finally, compare the results of each fund-raiser to determine which was most successful. Take it a step further by trying to figure out why. This ability to analyze situations carefully is a critical skill for a professional development officer.

COMPUTER BUCKS

As with so many other professions, the Internet is making work much easier for the professional fund-raiser. On the Net you can discover news about federal grants, research about corporate donors, and all kinds of pertinent data and statistics.

The first spot to visit is the National Endowment of the Arts home page at http://www.arts.endow.gov/. With links such as

Culture Quest, the Nonprofit Gateway, and Money for Individual Artists, you can find a gold mine of information about funding for arts organizations. From this spot, you can also find your way to arts-related organizations all over the country. Just click on the Arts Resources option.

Other sites to browse include the Smithsonian Museum, the National Gallery of Art, and any local arts and culture sites you can find with the help of your favorite Internet search engine. Also, run a word search on the specific areas of the arts that you have a special interest in—opera, ballet, performing arts, etc.

CHECK IT OUT

The following list suggests fund-raising–related organizations to contact.

The Foundation Center
79 Fifth Avenue, Eighth Floor
New York, New York 10003

Independent Sector
1828 L Street NW
Washington, D.C. 20036

National Academy on Volunteerism
701 North Fairfax Street
Alexandria, Virginia 22314-2045

National Society of Fund Raising Executives
1101 King Street, Suite 700
Alexandria, Virginia 22314
800-666-FUND

Nonprofit Management Association
1309 L Street NW
Washington, D.C. 20005

Below are listed arts-related organizations to contact.

American Association of Museums
1225 I Street NW, Suite 200
Washington, D.C. 20005

American Symphony Orchestra League
633 E Street NW
Washington, D.C. 20004

National Assembly of Local Arts Agencies
1420 K Street NW, Suite 204
Washington, D.C. 20005

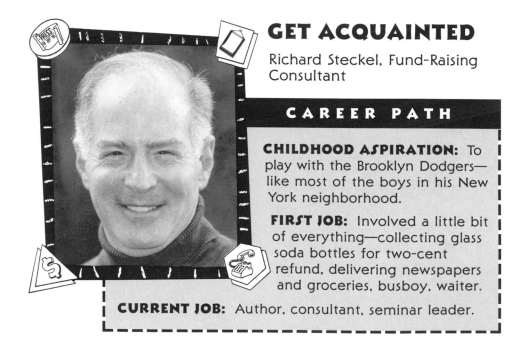

GET ACQUAINTED

Richard Steckel, Fund-Raising
Consultant

CAREER PATH

CHILDHOOD ASPIRATION: To play with the Brooklyn Dodgers—like most of the boys in his New York neighborhood.

FIRST JOB: Involved a little bit of everything—collecting glass soda bottles for two-cent refund, delivering newspapers and groceries, busboy, waiter.

CURRENT JOB: Author, consultant, seminar leader.

IF HE ONLY KNEW THEN . . .

When Richard Steckel looks back on his life, he notes several "magic moments" that forged his destiny. One occurred when he was just eight years old. He was so intrigued by a movie he watched about a shipwreck off the coast of Australia that he instinctively knew—whatever he did with his life—it had to involve international travel. So far, his work has taken him throughout the United States, Canada, Australia, Argentina, Chile, and Nigeria.

A second important event occurred when he was in eighth grade. He had a social studies teacher who was adored by all the girls. He liked the idea of being liked, so he decided to pursue a teaching degree in college.

Another life-altering experience occurred when he was a teenager. He saved up his own money from odd jobs to help reconstruct a church in Chile after an earthquake. This empowering experience made him realize that it was possible for one person to make a difference in others' lives.

One of his first adult jobs involving smuggling money from UNICEF to Nigeria for liberation groups in southern Africa. He later worked in the Ministry of Education in Canada.

COLORADO, HERE WE COME

Steckel's work in development took on a new dimension when he became director of the struggling Denver Children's Museum. It was there that he revolutionized the way nonprofit organizations support themselves. He developed marketing strategies that linked kid-friendly projects with corporate sponsors, staged some phenomenally successful special events (Trick or Treat Street is still a Denver favorite), and put some fun into fund-raising. You can read about these escapades in Steckel's book *Filthy Rich and Other Nonprofit Fantasies: Changing the Way Nonprofits Do Business in the 1990's* (Berkeley, Calif.: Ten Speed Press, 1988).

BE TRUE TO YOURSELF

Steckel's career reflects an interesting journey of involvement in the things that matter most to him. He grew up in the 1960s and found himself smack in the middle of the Civil Rights and anti–Vietnam War movements. Thus, his values were forged during a time of social upheaval.

As a result, he found that a core value for him was that his work advance more choices for people—in education, work, and overall quality of life. This value has been part of every career decision he's made.

IT'S A GREAT REASON TO GET UP IN THE MORNING

Development is one of those careers in which the more you care about the cause you are working for, the more successful you will be. Choose an area in which you'd gladly spend your free time, be it sports, opera, or charity. By approaching it this way, work moves beyond being just the "hired gun" to raise money; it lets you live and breathe the issue.

READY OR NOT!

If you feel strongly about something, even if it doesn't have a name, don't give up on it. The world may not be ready for your ideas yet. Hang in there, read, talk to people, and make choices that are best for you.

STECKEL'S DEC THEORY

Determination, enthusiasm, and curiosity are always valued. Keep these traits handy, and they'll take you places.

Fashion Designer

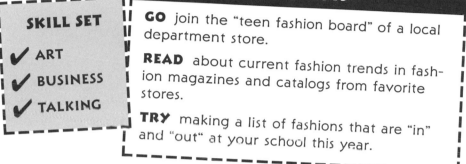

SHORTCUTS

GO join the "teen fashion board" of a local department store.

READ about current fashion trends in fashion magazines and catalogs from favorite stores.

TRY making a list of fashions that are "in" and "out" at your school this year.

WHAT IS A FASHION DESIGNER?

The clothes you are wearing right now say something about your attitude. They might be saying things like

- ☼ "I'm cool."
- ☼ "I couldn't care less."
- ☼ "I'm preppy."
- ☼ "Don't mess with me."

Whether you realize it or not, your fashion statements are the result of someone else's hard work. Fashion designers keep up on the latest trends and attitudes to design clothes that meet the needs of everyone from the newest baby to the oldest grandparent.

It takes a lot of people-watching and window-shopping to stay one step ahead of the next fashion craze. Fashion designers have to know what's hot and what's not. Since they are always working ahead toward the next season's fashions, they have to make careful distinctions (sometimes known as educated guesses) between last season's hits and next season's sensations.

Designers may work on anywhere between 50 and 150 designs for each season. Their work starts with detailed sketches of each design (either drawn by hand or by computer). The designer then makes pattern pieces for the garment (sometimes this is done by a pattern-maker or assistant). The pattern is used to cut carefully selected fabric to size in order to make a sample garment.

Samples are shown to buyers, and either the orders start rolling in or the designer goes back to the drawing board to incorporate suggested changes. The buying process often takes place at seasonal fashion shows.

There is an edge of glamour attached to this creative profession. However, fashion designers are just as likely to be employed designing the latest looks in underwear and children's play clothes as they are in the high-profile world of Paris couture. No matter what you're designing though, a career in fashion can be a creative way to put your artistic flair to good use.

Training for a career in fashion design usually involves attending an art school, a school specializing in fashion design, or a more traditional college or vocational/technical school offering a major in fashion design or textiles and clothing. A typical program will cover topics such as fashion development, consumer demand, fashion research and analysis, fabric production, apparel design development, and manufacturing processes. Of course, there will also be plenty of opportunity to hone your design skills.

You can start preparing yourself for this profession now by taking as many courses as you can in art (especially painting, sketching, sculpture, and screen printing), sewing, and computer-aided design (CAD). Psychology courses can also be useful in gaining a better understanding of human nature.

The fashion design industry is huge; in New York alone it does an estimated $14 billion in business per year. In a business this big, there's always room for fresh, new talent. Perhaps, you'll be the creative force behind the next big fashion trend.

TRY IT OUT

TRACK THE TRENDS

It's out with the old, in with the new. If you dream of becoming a designer, start training your eye for fashion now. Start keeping a fashion journal with sketches and clippings of the hottest looks for each season—spring and fall.

Date each entry and make sure to update the journal every year. By the time you graduate from high school, you are bound to have quite an interesting collecting of fashion's hits and misses.

SNEAK A PEEK AT THE LATEST FASHIONS

Fashion shows are an integral part of the fashion scene. Attend all that you can. Department stores can be good sources of seasonal trunk shows.

New York City, Chicago, Dallas, Atlanta, and Los Angeles are among the fashion manufacturing hot spots in the United States. Other cities specialize in specific areas of fashion. In Denver, it's skiwear, in Boston it's bridal gowns and accessories, and in Miami it's swimwear. Check your local phone book to locate manufacturers near you. The fashion pages of the local newspaper will also be a helpful source of information about fashion-related events in your area. Of course, if you get the chance to attend the big ones in New York or Paris, don't hesitate!

SKETCHES TO WEAR

The ultimate test of whether or not you should become a fashion designer is whether or not you can design fashions. Sketch ideas of clothes you'd like to wear. Use current fashions as a starting point, but remember, don't copy—create! Compile your best sketches in a scrapbook.

Then you might want to enlist the help of an accomplished seamstress (ask around among your friends or relatives) to make a sample of one of your designs. Better yet, learn to sew yourself (this is a must if you intend to go on to fashion school).

For ideas and inspiration visit the Fashion Planet website at http://www.fashion-planet.com. At this address you'll find the latest fashion news and gossip as well as updates on the latest trends and emerging looks.

MORE THAN MEETS THE EYE

The world of fashion offers an interesting array of career options. Some require extensive training and experience; others require a good dose of pluck and plenty of hard work. All require fashion sense and confidence in your abilities to make a contribution in a competitive field. Careers related to fashion design include manufacturer's representative, model, window display designer, fashion writer or photographer, accessory designer, fabric stylist, and costume designer.

You may find the following books particularly useful in helping sort out fashionable career options.

Beckett, Kathleen. *Careers Without College: Fashion*. Princeton, N.J.: Peterson's, 1992.

Black, Judy. *Careers in Fashion*. Morristown, N.J.: Silver Burdett Press, 1994.

Mauro, Lucia. *Careers for Fashion Plates and Other Trendsetters*. Lincolnwood, Ill.: VGM Career Horizons, 1996.

KEEP UP WITH THE INDUSTRY

Everybody who's anybody in the fashion world stays current by reading *Women's Wear Daily*. This newspaper provides up-to-the-minute accounts of every aspect of the fashion industry five days a week.

Subscriptions are pricey, making the search for a library with a subscription an especially appealing option. For more information on subscribing, write to *Women's Wear Daily*, P.O. Box 10531, Riverton, New Jersey 08706-0531, or call 800-289-0273.

You can also get a sneak peak of an issue and access a database of upcoming fashion and apparel trade shows on the Internet at http://www.wwd.com.

CYBERFASHION

As part of the Smithsonian Institution, New York's Cooper-Hewitt National Design Museum is home to an extensive collection of drawings, prints, decorative arts, textiles, and wall coverings. Wander through some of the world's best design work by linking up with the museum's website at http://www.si.edu/ndm/.

TIPS FROM THE TOP

If you are really serious about a career in fashion design, you might want to purchase a copy of "the Career Counseling Workbook" put out by The Fashion Group International. In it, you'll find information on preparing résumés and cover letters, some insightful self-evaluation exercises, and an expertly compiled recruiter list (all you need to know about applying for work with some of the bigger fashion firms). Since the workbook is compiled by a team of fashion "insiders," you can expect to find information not readily available elsewhere. To order a copy, contact The Fashion Group International, Inc., 597 Fifth Avenue, Eighth Floor, New York, New York 10017.

CHECK IT OUT

American Apparel
  Manufacturer's Association
2500 Wilson Boulevard
Arlington, Virginia 22201

American Sewing Guild
P.O. Box 8568
Medford, Oregon 97504

Clothing Manufacturer's Association
1290 Avenue of the Americas
New York, New York 10104

Council of Fashion Designers
   of America
1412 Broadway, Suite 1714
New York, New York 10018

Fashion Group International
597 Fifth Avenue, Eighth Floor
New York, New York 10017

International Association of
   Clothing Design
240 Madison Avenue, 12th Floor
New York, New York 10016

Men's Fashion Associations
   of America
240 Madison Avenue
New York, New York 10016

National Outerwear and
   Sportswear Association
240 Madison Avenue
New York, New York 10016

United Garment Workers of
   America
4207 Lebanon Road
Hermitage, Tennessee 37076

GET ACQUAINTED

June Beckstead, Fashion Designer

CAREER PATH

CHILDHOOD ASPIRATION: To be a veterinarian. She had 24 hamsters at one time to prove it!

FIRST JOB: Selling clothes at a retail shop.

CURRENT JOB: Vice president of women's product design for the Gap, Inc.

WHEN ONE PLUS ONE EQUALS FASHION

June Beckstead had always enjoyed art as a child. She briefly lost touch with her artistic talent in high school. However, she discovered another creative area that she really enjoyed when she started working in a clothing store.

When she graduated from high school, Beckstead was inde-
cisive about her future. During a heart-to-heart talk, her father
encouraged her to think about what she liked to do. She liked
art; she liked clothes. Put the two together, and you've got a
career in fashion.

To this day, Beckstead is grateful that her father had the
insight to guide her toward her talent and interests.

OFF AND RUNNING

Beckstead earned a degree in fashion design from the Fashion
Institute of Technology and started her career by freelancing
for a small award-winning company. Starting in a small company proved invaluable because it gave Beckstead a chance
to learn about every aspect of the business: the design room,
the pattern room, the show room, and the public relations
side of things.

The only downside to this experience was that she couldn't
walk into a store and find the clothes. Having moved on to bigger companies, she gets a real kick out of seeing her clothes on
the street every day.

GETTING READY FOR A NEW SEASON

With her team, Beckstead is responsible for designing seasonal
lines of women's clothing that typically include some 100
sweaters as well as 100 knit items, and 100 woven pieces
(including all the different colors and patterns for each piece).
Beckstead's team of designers and stylists has about two to
three months to develop each season's line.

As the person in charge of the team responsible for the
success of the line, Beckstead has to know what's happening
in the fashion world. To keep up with what's hot, she visits
Europe two or three times each year and always keeps an eye
on what people are wearing in places such as New York, Los
Angeles, and selected college campuses (a big segment of
her company's market).

Ultimately, her fashion decisions come back to staying true
to her customer. Gap customers expect a certain look. Even
the latest trends have to be reinterpreted to suit these expec-

tations. When the line is a hit, she has more than 800 stores across the country to share the success. If something turns out to be a dud, the same 800-plus stores wonder why their cash registers aren't ringing.

There is pressure, but Beckstead thrives on the fast pace.

A VOICE OF EXPERIENCE

A strong portfolio is a must for getting anywhere in the fashion industry. Beckstead has these tips for making sure your portfolio is noticed.

- Include at least 15 illustrations—well-mounted and professionally displayed—of designs using either male or female figures.
- Make sure the designs "tell a story" with a beginning, middle, and end. The story should involve coordinating fabric and seasonal themes.
- Show an understanding of the manufacturing process by including flat sketches of the front and back of each design, illustrating even the tiniest details such as seams and buttons.
- Demonstrate where you found the inspiration for your designs by putting together a "mood board" with tearsheets from magazines, postcards, fabric swatches, and any other sources of ideas.

In the end, it's your portfolio and your persistence that will sell your skill as a fashion designer.

Floral Designer

SHORTCUTS

GO ask if you can help around a local flower shop to get the hang of things. If you really like it and do good work, you may land yourself a job.

READ gardening magazines—supermarkets, bookstores, and newsstands have many fun choices. Pick one that appeals to you.

TRY arranging a centerpiece for the dinner table. Either buy a few fresh flowers and some greens from the florist or go outside and see what kind of creative ingredients you can come up with.

WHAT IS A FLORAL DESIGNER?

Floral designers play a part in people's best days and worst days. Their work helps people celebrate the high points in life and offers comfort during the low points of life. Weddings, birthdays, holidays, and funerals are just a few of the occasions when flowers are used as an expression of celebration or condolence. If you've ever been the recipient of a surprise bouquet, you know how effective flowers can be.

If doing your own thing creatively appeals to you, it may be worth your while to find out more about this profession. Whether it's with fresh, dried, or silk flowers, floral designers (or florists) use flowers to create moods, communicate important messages, and enliven the everyday lives of others. If you want your artistic ability to be noticed and appreciated, being a florist is a great way to do it. A beautiful flower arrangement is guaranteed to be the center of attention in any room.

Floral designers often work for retail stores that specialize in producing and delivering flower arrangements. Sometimes they also own the stores and must incorporate keen business management skills into their daily responsibilities. Others specialize in special events, such as weddings and big parties, and work directly for bridal shops, catering companies, or even funeral homes. Freelance designers succeed by developing good working relationships with wedding and event planners. Some flower aficionados actually grow flowers in nurseries or on flower farms. Others sell flowers wholesale to retail shops, acting as liaison, or middleman, between the growers and the sellers. It is becoming increasingly common for florists to work in supermarkets, serving as designers, buyers, and shop managers. This arrangement can offer a satisfying mix of variety and experience. Another related profession involves the care and feeding of plant life in public places and/or offices.

The profession obviously demands a thorough knowledge of flowers coupled with a sense of color and design. For those who operate their own shops or nurseries, strong business skills are a must too.

There are no formal training requirements for floral designers. The nature of the work lends itself to on-the-job training or an apprenticeship (a formal on-site training situation where you learn from an experienced designer). For those who prefer a more structured training program, flower arranging courses can be found through some flower shops or continuing education programs.

Those designers who hope to one day own their own shops may want to consider pursuing a special certification through a community college or commercial floral design school. These programs typically offer courses in horticulture, marketing, and business management, as well as more intensive training in floral design.

Floral design is an appealing option for those looking for both a means of artistic expression and a means of helping others. The work is fairly evenly paced, although things can get hectic around certain holidays. Of course, spending your workday surrounded by beautiful flowers can also be a definite plus.

TRY IT OUT

A PICTURE IS WORTH A THOUSAND WORDS

Look through some old magazines and cut out pictures of all the different flower arrangements you can find. Paste each picture to a separate sheet of paper. Use the following questions (recommended by the prestigious Rittner's Floral School) to critique each arrangement from an artist's point of view.

- What shape is the design?
- How many flowers are in the design?
- What kinds of flowers are in the design?
- What occasion is the design for?
- Where do you think a design like this would be best placed?
- What colors are in the piece?
- How are the colors placed?
- Is the floral design

  formal?   contemporary?
  informal?   seasonal?
  traditional?
- Does the floral design evoke a mood? If so, how?
- How do you feel about the floral art? Do you like it? Why?

BOTANICAL CRASH COURSE

While you still have those magazines and scissors handy, use them to find pictures of specific types of flowers. Paste each picture on a separate page in a notebook. Use a library book on botany or flowers to identify each variety. Label each picture with both its common and scientific name. Use the margin to jot down notes about other facts you discover about each flower (for example, special care instructions, native habitat, or traditions associated with the flower).

Just for fun, you may also want to learn the language of flowers. Flowers don't talk in actual words, but they certainly communicate very specific messages. Nothing says love quite like a rose. So, if a carnation represents joy, which flower represents hope?

After you've learned all you can about as many flowers as you can, make a visit to a flower shop and get better acquainted with these newfound friends. Notice the smell, the texture, and the leaves. Memorize every detail. All this advance training will go a long way to impress a potential employer someday!

AN ON-LINE FLORIST SCHOOL

The website for Rittner's School of Floral Design in Boston includes some fun and practical information about floral designing as a career. In fact, the school's site provides an insider's perspective on this profession, including tips on opportunities and a realistic look at the pros and cons. In addition, the school's site has links to other floral resources on the Internet. And, if that weren't enough to warrant a visit, it also provides a free Internet introduction to the basics of floral design. Options for learning include topics such as simple line arrangement, how to make a mound, arranging flowers in vases, and more. You can access all this information at http://www.tiac.net/users/stevrt/index.html.

MARY, MARY QUITE CONTRARY

How does your garden grow? Growing your own garden can be a wonderful way to cultivate a relationship with flowers. It doesn't matter if you start with a flower pot or an entire plot of land, get some seeds and start planting!

CHECK IT OUT

Florists Transworld Delivery Association
29200 Northwestern Highway
Southfield, Michigan 48034

Rittner's School of Floral Design
345 Marlborough Street
Boston, Massachusetts 02115

Society of American Florists
1601 Duke Street
Alexandria, Virginia 22314

GET ACQUAINTED

Rebecca Black, Flower Grower
and Designer

CAREER PATH

CHILDHOOD ASPIRATION: To
be in business for herself.

FIRST JOB: Fashion model as a
teen and after high school.

CURRENT JOB: Owner of
Foxglove Farm.

Rebecca Black not only designs incredible dried flower arrangements, wreaths, and garlands, but she grows the flowers too! She lives in a century-old Canadian manor, built by Russian immigrants, and grows 17 acres of flowers on the estate grounds.

Once the flowers reach the peak of perfection, she and her staff harvest them and hang them to dry in an enormous ballroom in the main house amid the grand piano and crystal chandeliers. The former gatekeeper's cottage serves as a year-round shop. If it all sounds a bit like a fairytale, it should. Her career is a dream come true for Black.

IT STARTED WITH AN IDEA

Black first grew flowers in a small garden for fun. One fall evening, she was arranging some of her homegrown flowers with some that she'd bought from the store. When she noticed that the store-bought flowers were already faded, she realized that she could do better a job. She started toying with the idea of a flower farm, did some research, plowed up the fields, and Foxglove Farm was born.

TAKE WHAT YOU HAVE AND MAKE IT WORK

There's been no stopping her since then. Sure, she's made a few mistakes along the way, but she's learned what she could from them and kept on moving forward. Although she's had no formal schooling in farming or botany, she's used common sense to discover what grows best in her region, which flowers keep their shape and color when dried, and what people want to buy.

People come from all over Canada to visit her farm, picnic, and take classes on the art of flower arranging.

REAP WHAT YOU SOW

Hard work, natural talent, exceptional product, and quality service are what Black brings to the marketplace. The result is a harvest of success and a lifestyle that dreams are made of.

Graphic Designer

WHAT IS A GRAPHIC DESIGNER?

Imagine that you receive two equally important pieces of mail. It is obvious that one was typed up quickly (the misspelled words are a dead giveaway) and printed out on a cheap dot matrix printer. Some of the words are smudged, and to make it even harder to read, it looks like a bad copy of a pretty bad original.

In contrast, the other piece is printed on thick, glossy paper. It even feels good. Bright colors and exciting visuals jump out, practically shouting, "Read me!"

The piece includes headlines, bullets, and other graphic elements that make it easy to scan, guaranteeing that you'll notice the important details.

Which one of these two documents would you read first? It's entirely possible (and quite likely) that you'd throw away the first one before even looking at it. It doesn't demand your attention like the second one does. Even though the first piece contains information that is every bit as important as the second one, it would likely be completely ignored.

Why is that? We live in a visual age, and we require color, style, and pizzazz to get and keep our attention.

This is very good news for graphic designers, because their job is to provide the look for all kinds of materials, making sure they get seen, read, and remembered. Good graphic design can make a lasting impact. If you don't believe it, just take the following little quiz. See if you can think of the company behind the following elements:

- golden arches? (Answer: McDonalds)
- multicolored apple? (Answer: Apple computers)
- big swoosh mark? (Answer: Nike athletic shoes)

These are examples of corporate logos. They help provide visual identity for big and small corporations. The goal is that when we see the logo, we instantly associate it with the company and its products (of course, the real goal is that we eventually buy something from the company, but that's another story).

Logos are just one way that graphic designers use a keen sense of artistic style combined with a working knowledge of various elements of design to create visually memorable materials. These same techniques are applied to book jackets, magazine and newspaper layouts, restaurant menus, and even weekly grocery store advertisements.

While natural artistic ability is helpful, an eye for design is a skill that can be learned, and in a variety of settings. Excellent training programs can be found at every level from trade school to graduate school. You may even find that your high school offers computer graphics classes.

Before you decide how much schooling you'll need, you'll have to decide what kind of specialty you want to pursue. A few graphic arts specialties to consider include

animator	fashion illustrator	science illustrator
art director	medical illustrator	textile designer
cartoonist	multimedia designer	video designer
desktop publisher	publication designer	

In addition to offering an appealing variety of specialties, graphic design is a profession that offers a number of employment options. It probably won't surprise you to learn that many graphic designers work for marketing and advertising companies. However, they also work in publishing houses, manufacturing firms, department stores, and government agencies. Computers and other high-tech equipment have made self-employment or freelancing a lucrative option for many an experienced and well-connected graphic designer.

If you want to use your artistic talent to beautify the things people read for business, education, or entertainment, graphic arts is a field to consider.

TRY IT OUT

WHEN YOU CARE ENOUGH TO SEND THE VERY BEST

One Internet spot worth a visit is the website for Hallmark cards. In addition to all kinds of interesting information about the company, it includes valuable insight into creative careers from an employer's perspective. Check it out at http://www.hallmark.com.

EVERYTHING YOU WANT TO KNOW ABOUT A CAREER IN GRAPHIC DESIGN

The American Institute of Graphic Arts publishes *Graphic Design: A Career Guide and Education Directory*, which includes information on almost everything there is to know about graphic design careers. It gives descriptions of more than

300 schools that offer four-year degrees in graphic design, defines the purpose and practice of the profession, suggests ways to evaluate schools and potential employers, and presents noteworthy projects to provide a visual orientation to the various aspects of the profession.

Copies are not free, so check with your school's career center first to see if they might order one for the school. The Institute's address is included in the Check It Out list below.

DESIGN A CAREER

If you are in hot pursuit of a career as a graphic designer, you'll want to find a copy of *Careers by Design: A Headhunter's Secrets for Success and Survival in Graphic Design* by Roz Goldfarb (New York: Allworth Press, 1993). This book provides a thorough (and interesting) introduction to some of the major graphic design specialties: corporate design, print design, promotional design, environmental design, industrial design, and computer design. It also includes information about building a portfolio and finding a good job.

While you read it, design a chart that lets you compare the various specialties at a glance. You'll want to include things like the required skills, training needs, and potential employers.

THE GOOD, THE BAD, AND THE AWFUL

Eventually, you'll need your own portfolio as a graphic designer. For now, you can learn a lot from the work of other graphic designers. You'll need to go only as far as your family's mailbox or stack of magazines for ideas.

Paste a variety of different kinds of written communications—everything from advertisements to greeting cards to a club newsletter—on large pieces of paper. Use a marker to list the best and worst features of each design. Take note of things like color, the use of different types of letters (called fonts), pictures, the kind of paper. What catches your eye? Is it a pleasure to look at or is it cluttered and confusing?

Keep your collection in a notebook or folder, organized in order from your favorite design to your not so favorite ones.

CHECK IT OUT

American Center for Design
Student Programs
233 East Ontario, Suite 500
Chicago, Illinois 60611

American Institute of
  Graphic Arts
1059 Third Avenue
New York, New York 10021

Art Director's Club, Inc.
250 Park Avenue South
New York, New York 10003

Association of Medical Illustrators
1819 Peachtree Street NE,
  Suite 560
Atlanta, Georgia 30309-1848

Graphic Artists Guild, Inc.
11 West 20th Street, Eighth Floor
New York, New York 10010

Graphic Design Education
  Association
North Carolina State University
Box 7701
Raleigh, North Carolina 27695

Guild of Natural Science Illustrators
P.O. Box 652, Ben Franklin Station
Washington, D.C. 20044-0652

Packaging Designers Council
P.O. Box 1332
Pleasant Valley, New York 12569

Society of Environmental
  Graphic Designers
1 Story Street
Cambridge, Massachusetts 02138

Society of Publication Designers
60 East 42nd Street, Suite 721
New York, New York 10165-1416

GET ACQUAINTED

Gary Pettit, Graphic Designer

CAREER PATH

CHILDHOOD ASPIRATION: To
be a musician.

FIRST JOB: Acting in summer
stock theater from age four.

CURRENT JOB: Visual design
director at Starwest Productions,
a family-owned corporation.

IT ALL STARTED WITH THE THREE LITTLE PIGS

Gary Pettit has always been good in art. He recalls a first-grade drawing assignment that the teacher hung on the wall. Even then, his drawing of the Three Little Pigs showed promise.

The funny thing is that he spent a good deal of his youth immersed in art and various forms of the arts (his whole family was musically inclined and had the acting bug). Yet Pettit never dreamed it would result in a profession, until one thing led to another, people started paying him for his work, and a great business was (almost accidentally) launched.

PETTIT'S FIFTEEN MINUTES OF FAME

The three Pettit brothers—Steve, Phil, and Gary—sang together as a trio and appeared on a number of stages throughout the Rocky Mountain region. They also made some radio commercials. Their claim to fame, however, was producing a record album to help raise money for crippled children. It didn't seem like such a big deal then, but Pettit recognizes the experience as one of those rare and wonderful opportunities in life.

A FAMILY AFFAIR

Today, Pettit, with his two brothers and their parents, runs a thriving business that utilizes everyone's best skills. Phil is the computer whiz, Steve is the creative director, and Gary rounds things off with his artistic expertise. Dad is a semiretired mechanical engineer but is always available for advice and ideas. Mom is the office manager and keeps everyone in line.

A LITTLE OF THIS, A LITTLE OF THAT

Pettit applies his creative genius to a variety of projects from developing logos and point-of-sale materials for an up-and-coming beverage company to developing promotional campaigns to generate excitement (and ticket sales) about new movies for a national chain of theaters. He also spends a good deal of time on sports marketing materials, designing posters, video clips, traveling exhibitions, and much more.

TOP OF THE LINE PRODUCTIONS

Whether he works in film, video, multi-image, display materials, or print, Pettit has built a solid reputation for producing some good stuff. So good, in fact, that his work has been honored with awards from national organizations such as the Public Relations Society of America, the Institute of Real Estate Management, the International Association of Business Communicators, the Association for Multi-Image, and the Chicago International Film Festival.

A PART OF THE COMMUNITY

The Pettit family has lived in Colorado for a couple generations. Metro Denver is home, and life there has been good to them. That's just one of the reasons why they donate a good portion of their time and talent to support causes that they believe in. Whether it's putting together an incredibly scary haunted house to earn money for a favorite charity or designing a newsletter to get the word out about a shelter for victims of abuse, Pettit follows a family tradition of making a contribution to his community.

IT'S NOT OVER TILL IT'S OVER

The Pettit brothers share a common, as yet unrealized, dream— to develop their own theme park. They have lots of great ideas and all sorts of plans; they just need someone with the land and money to back the project. It's proved an illusive dream so far. At one point, they were within inches of cutting the big deal when things fell apart. Like all worthwhile dreams, this one is worth waiting for.

Industrial Designer

SKILL SET

✔ ART

✔ MATH

✔ SCIENCE

GO put together anything you can get your hands on to learn the logic behind the way things are constructed. Puzzles, model airplanes, dollhouses, old clocks are a few ideas to get you started.

READ David Macaulay's book *The Way Things Work.*

TRY thinking up ideas for a "better mousetrap."

WHAT IS AN INDUSTRIAL DESIGNER?

"Design is the way something looks and how it works. It's art. It's technology. It's an object, or group of objects. It's a plan, a sketch, a drawing. Something decorative, something functional. A pattern, a model, an invention. It's also a process: to think, plan, conceive, form, create, make, build, envision. Design is work. And play. A part of everyone's life. A measure of the quality of life."

That's how a brochure about the National Design Museum sums up the design process. This museum houses some 30,000 three-dimensional applied arts and industrial design artifacts, from ancient times to present day.

The museum's official definition of an industrial design is "the professional service of creating and developing concepts and specifications that optimize the function, value and appearance of products and systems for the mutual benefit of both user and manufacturer." In other words, it is the design of products manufactured by industrial processes.

The creative ideas of an industrial designer are behind some of your favorite everyday things: CDs and CD players, laptop computers, cellular phones, microwave ovens, and big screen TVs, among other things. They all went through an intensive design process before you found them at the store. The desk and chair you use at school, those cool new halogen lamps, disposable razors, bicycle helmets—all are the result of an innovative industrial designer.

An industrial designer is part artist, part engineer, part inventor. Add a touch of the philosopher and a bit of business executive, and you'll have the perfect mix for an effective industrial designer. The industrial designer uses technology to solve real world problems. He or she relies on customer research to design products that people need and want to buy.

According to the Industrial Designers Society of America (IDSA), industrial designers must know how to work with their heads as well as their hands. They must learn to see solutions where others see problems. They must know something about everything, as well as a lot about building things and making things happen.

Industrial designers are playing an increasingly important role in developing products that either take the market by storm or become long-running mainstays. Products such as the Apple PowerBook, Gillette's Sensor razor, and Reebok's Pump sneaker are examples of such hot sellers.

Industrial designers are just as likely to start their education at an art college or school of design as they are to start at a major university. A good industrial design training program is similar to an engineering program, with courses in mathematics, physics, and economics. The program should progressively introduce opportunities to apply one's growing knowledge to projects—making drawings, models, full-scale mock-ups, and eventually simulated finished projects. Internships and on-the-job training are particularly useful in this field.

So much in our world is affected by the design process. Everything from automobiles to zippers can use creative design to become more efficient, more environmentally friendly, and more cost-effective. Some product out there may be waiting for your creative input!

TRY IT OUT

AND THE WINNER IS . . .

The Industrial Designers Society of America presents annual industrial design awards in the areas of business and industrial products, consumer products, design exploration, environmental design, furniture, packaging and design, transportation, and medical and scientific design. These categories should give you an idea of how broad the applications in this field are.

To find out about current winners or for an application to submit a student entry, contact IDSA at the address listed in the Check It Out section. IDSA can also be contacted by e-mail at idsa@erols.com, or visit IDSA at http://www.idsa.org.

GET THE INSIDE STORY

Houghton Mifflin produces *Inventor Labs*, a CD-ROM encyclopedia of great inventions. With it you get the chance to explore more than 40 three-dimensional inventions by some of the greatest inventors of all time, such as Thomas Edison and Alexander Graham Bell. The CD takes you inside their historically accurate re-created laboratories and through their experiments.

For more information contact Houghton Mifflin Interactive, 120 Beacon Street, Sommerville, Massachusetts 02142, or visit their website at http://www.hmco.com.

VIRTUAL IDEAS

The next time you go on-line, you'll want to stop by the website of the Cooper-Hewitt National Design Museum. Of particular interest is the Department of Applied Arts and Industrial Design. Part of the prestigious Smithsonian Institute, the museum focuses on design as it relates to architecture, environmental design, graphic design, and industrial design. The site contains a wealth of information as well as links to other design-related sites. The address is http://www.si.edu/organiza/museums/design/start.htm.

Another stop you'll want to make is to Design Online (http://www.dol.com), an award-winning site that features a library of design ideas as well as a design compass to other sites. And before you sign off, visit the American Institute of Graphic Arts' virtual gallery. The address is http://www.aiga.org/.

CHECK IT OUT

American Society of Furniture Designers
P.O. Box 2688
High Point, North Carolina 27261

Industrial Designers Society of America
1142 Walker Road, Suite E
Great Falls, Virginia 22066

Institute of Industrial Engineering
25 Technology Park/Atlanta
Norcross, Georgia 10017

National Association of Schools of Art and Design
11250 Roger Bacon Drive, Suite 21
Reston, Virginia 22066

Plastics Institute of America
277 Fairfield Road, Suite 100
Fairfield, New Jersey 07004-1932

GET ACQUAINTED
Anthony Grieder,
Industrial Designer

CAREER PATH

CHILDHOOD ASPIRATION: To become an architect.

FIRST JOB: Shipping clerk in a roll bar factory.

CURRENT JOB: Project director of industrial design for Volan Design, LLC.

THE CLUES WERE THERE ALL ALONG

As a child, Anthony Grieder spent his spare time building intricate towns and buildings for little toy animals. Things got so elaborate that his family eventually had to set aside an entire room in the house for him to pursue this hobby.

As is so often the case, this childhood passion provided the groundwork for his ultimate career as an industrial designer. Now instead of dreaming up suitable habitats for rubber toys, he applies the same kind of careful, logical thinking to dreaming up new products for clients.

THE BEST DECISION HE'S EVER MADE

After deciding there wasn't much money to be made as a professional trombone player, Grieder pursued his childhood ambition of becoming an architect. He earned a bachelor's degree in environmental design and then spent the summer working for a distant relative's architectural firm in South Africa.

The only problem was that to Grieder the work was boring. He found himself separated from the creative process by tons of details and layers of architects with lots more experience than he had.

Desperately in need of a new plan, he decided to go for a master's degree in product design. He says it's the best decision he's ever made. Now, instead of spending laborious hours on little details, he has seen some of his great ideas come to be a reality.

His first job on his new path as a designer involved helping design upscale shopping centers. Everything from the furniture and lighting to each of the storefronts was customized to make for a unique shopping experience. He started out as low man on the project, so he spent a lot of time constructing models that represented each idea—shades of childhood past!

THE DOCTOR IS IN

In recent years, Grieder has specialized in designing medical equipment as well as products for the health club industry. One of his products won award of excellence from the Rocky Mountain Chapter of the Industrial Designers Society of America (IDSA). The product, an attachment to pulse oximeters, was designed to save hundreds of feet of cable wire. The result was a huge savings in money and resources.

Other products that Grieder has had a hand in designing include a machine that pitches Wiffle-type balls, a cross-country ski machine, and a machine combining a stair-climber and a treadmill for health clubs.

IN HIS DREAMS

Underneath Grieder's calm exterior lives a car fanatic. His dream project would involve designing some unique features for a truck or sports car.

BEST ADVICE

According to Grieder there are a couple things a young person can do now to start preparing for a career in industrial design. One is to read magazines about specialized products such as cars, computers, motorcycles, etc. That's a good way to learn about the business and to cultivate an area of specialization.

Another all-important tip is: Get good grades in school! Work hard now, and there will be more opportunities for you later.

Above all, always be open to new ideas. You never know where they'll take you.

Interior Designer

SHORTCUTS

SKILL SET

✔ ART

✔ BUSINESS

✔ TALKING

GO visit historic homes and garden shows.

READ *Architectural Digest, House and Garden, Southern Living,* and *Accent* magazines for the latest information on new products and fresh ideas.

TRY making detailed sketches of each room in your house.

WHAT IS AN INTERIOR DESIGNER?

What do you think about a traditional approach? Maybe a more contemporary look is more to your liking? How about making things a bit cozier with a French country touch? Should you use chintz or a nice moiré to cover the sofa? Roman shades or wood shutters for the window?

All these choices and details make interior design a challenging and exciting profession. According to group consensus of several professional associations, the official definition for an interior designer is one who is "qualified by education, experience, and examination to enhance the function and quality of interior spaces."

This is done "for the purpose of improving the quality of life, increasing productivity, and protecting the health, safety, and welfare of the public."

That means that interior designers decorate people's homes and public places. Some designers specialize in design for specific spaces, such as

- ☼ businesses, offices, and industrial workplaces
- ☼ restaurants, hotels, resorts, and spas
- ☼ hospitals and other medical facilities
- ☼ retail stores, malls, displays, or exhibits
- ☼ churches, synagogues, and other places of worship
- ☼ schools and college campuses
- ☼ museums and theaters
- ☼ government facilities—including everything from the local post office to the White House
- ☼ transportation—trains, ships, airplanes, submarines, and spaceships

Still other interior designers specialize in set design—for theater, television, and movies—or in lighting design. Teaching, illustration, product development, and historic preservation are other outlets for the creative interior designer.

No matter what kind of space is involved, the process usually begins by discussing options with the client. The designer must listen carefully and ask the right questions to get an idea of what the client hopes to achieve in the space. Next, the designer sketches or uses a computer to draw pictures of various ideas. The sketch includes the furniture, special built-in features in the room, fabrics, colors, and the overall theme. The designer must be very careful to draw all elements to scale, making sure that they accurately represent the space.

Once a concept is approved, the designer must work with manufacturers, builders, and other workers to find all the materials and products necessary to carry out the design. This is where knowing who's who and what's what comes in very handy. A successful interior designer is a carefully balanced mixture of super shopper, detective, and supervisor. Sometimes items can be purchased directly from a manufacturer; other times they have to be built to very detailed specifications. In every case, the designer must know the best and most affordable source of securing every single item needed to meet the design plan.

The process requires attention to every detail, thorough knowledge of design concepts, great contacts with suppliers, and a vivid imagination for conjuring up all the possibilities.

Though not rigidly required, professional training is generally expected. Interior design schools and some art schools offer three-year certification programs. Many colleges and universities offer four-year bachelor's degree programs. Wherever the education is obtained, an aspiring interior designer can expect to take courses in art history, architectural drawing and drafting, fine arts, and furniture design. Other courses will cover topics such as lighting, electrical equipment, and communication and business skills.

Although it is not necessary to obtain a license, working toward professional accreditation can be an asset in this field. Accreditation involves meeting specific training and experience guidelines and passing a national examination administered by the National Council for Interior Design Qualification. Upon meeting these criteria, a designer becomes eligible for membership in participating professional associations.

Interior designers help keep the world beautiful. They add zest and charm and comfort to the places where people live, work, and play. Their work involves an exciting mix of artistic expression and people-pleasing skills. The work is both creative and demanding.

TRY IT OUT

A MAKEOVER YOU CAN SLEEP IN

It doesn't have to cost a lot of money to update your own personal space. In fact, you'll be surprised to see what rearranging the furniture and decorations can do for any room. Begin with your own bedroom.

First, make a plan. Use chart paper to experiment with different ways to arrange the furniture. Then, look through books and decorating magazines for ideas on color schemes. Browse through the home furnishings and bed and bathroom sections of department stores at the mall for further inspiration. Another good place to look for cost-cutting ideas is a fabric shop. Pattern books are full of fairly simple and inexpensive ideas for sprucing up the home.

If time, resources, and your parents allow, take the process a little further by updating the color, window coverings, and bedspread.

PAINT YOUR DREAM HOUSE IN LIVING COLOR

Pick out a pretty photo album filled with plenty of pages for mounting pictures. Designate a page or two for each room you hope to have in your ultimate dream house. Be sure to leave space for each bedroom and bathroom.

Make it a habit to thumb through every magazine you come across looking for decorating ideas. When you find a picture of something particularly appealing, clip it and put it in the appropriate spot in your planning album. Feel free to add sketches of your own and notes that describe the features that you like best.

COMPUTERIZED DECORATING

As with so many other industries, computers have revolutionized the way interior designers work. They make it easier to prepare detailed plans, track supplies, and monitor expenses. Try your hand at computerized decorating with one of the following programs.

- Design It! software by SoftKey International offers a fun and easy way to bring your decorating ideas to life with interactive three-dimensional graphics. Order directly from the company by calling 800-845-8692 or pick up a copy at a software store.
- 3-D Home Interiors software by Broderbund includes more than 100,000 brand-name appliances and fur-

nishing that you can "pop" into your designs with a click of a button. It also includes a portfolio of professional designs and an option for tracking the project budget. Order directly from the company by calling 800-521-1809 or pick up a copy at a software store.

DECORATING BY THE BOOK

You'll find decorating books by the dozens at the local library. The 747 section includes books on all aspects of decorating—basic decorating techniques, furniture styles, fabric, glassware, etc. Learn some interior design basics in books such as

---

Gilliatt, Mary. *The Decorating Book.* New York: Pantheon, 1981.

———. *Decorating on the Cheap: Designer's Secrets and Tricks of the Trade.* New York: Workman Publishing, 1984.

Moss, Charlotte. *Decorating a Room: A Designer's Guide to Decorating Your Home in Stages.* New York: Viking Penguin, 1995.

CHECK IT OUT

American Society for Interior Designers
608 Massachusetts Avenue NE
Washington, D.C. 20002

Environmental Design Research Association, Inc.
P.O. Box 24083
Oklahoma City, Oklahoma 73124

Foundation for Interior Design Education Research
60 Monroe Center NW
Grand Rapids, Michigan 49503

Institute of Business Designers
1115 Merchandise Mart
Chicago, Illinois 60654

Interior Design Educators Council
14252 Culver Drive, Suite A-311
Irvine, California 92714

Interior Designers of Canada
160 Pears Avenue, Suite 207
Toronto, Ontario M5R 1T2

International Society of Interior Designers
433 South Spring Street, Suite 6-D
Los Angeles, California 92714

National Council for Interior Design Qualification
118 East 25th Street
New York, New York 10010

GET ACQUAINTED

Kaki Hockersmith,
Interior Designer

CAREER PATH

CHILDHOOD ASPIRATION: To be an actress or writer.

FIRST JOB: Working in her dad's advertising agency.

CURRENT JOB: Runs her own interior design firm.

MAKING THE MOST OF EVERY OPPORTUNITY

Kaki Hockersmith never really intended to become an interior designer. She went to college and earned a double major in English and history with a double minor in speech and art. Then she graduated, got married, and became a schoolteacher. She taught for a while, but when she was offered the chance to help produce an educational history series for the local public television affiliate, she jumped at it.

After that project was over, a long-time friend offered her a position as a designer for a chain of fashionable department stores. Always willing to keep her options open, Hockersmith accepted the position. Her job was to decorate the "vignettes" (those little rooms) in the furniture departments. She had to plan the color scheme and accessories, decide how to arrange the furniture, and make sure that each of the stores had everything they needed to put it together. In this job, she learned the ropes of interior design and discovered she had a natural talent for the work.

She eventually started her own decorating business in Little Rock, Arkansas. She says she learned as she went along and sometimes wished she had professional training in the field. She worked hard and paid some hard dues in the process.

However, it all paid off when she won the commission to redecorate the governor's mansion in Arkansas. The governor at the time was Bill Clinton. He and his family so liked the comfortable English country look that she gave the family quarters that when they moved to Washington, D.C., they asked Hockersmith to serve as their official decorator.

A HOUSE IS A HOUSE (OR IS IT?)

While it's pretty exciting to be asked to decorate the White House, Hockersmith found the process to be similar to any other project. Her basic plan stayed the same: Consider the client's needs, consider the client's preferences, and consider how the room is used. The finished room is deemed a success only when all three of these standards are met.

Of course, the White House offered some important, historic considerations as well. Not every house has first picking in a warehouse filled with 40,000 square feet of museum-quality art and antiques. And not every project involves hordes of reporters following your every move and other famous designers analyzing every element of the design. The pressure was high and so were the stakes.

Fortunately for Hockersmith, the finished results are widely considered a smashing success. Her clients, President and Mrs. Clinton, were very pleased with the new look, and with her newfound fame, her career suddenly took on a global feel. Clients from all over the world sought her out. Hockersmith, however, remains closely connected with the White House as a presidential appointee to the Committee for the Preservation of the White House, an honor that affords her the opportunity to work in historic preservation on a grand scale.

HOCKERSMITH WAS HERE

Hockersmith works very carefully to make sure that each project she completes accurately reflects the tastes of her clients. She hopes never to become so boring that a person could immediately identify something as the Hockersmith signature style. There is only one thing that consistently marks every project she works on, and that is her attention to detail. She puts a lot of attention and planning into creating looks that look unplanned. Her goal in any space is to make it "real" and create a sense that somebody actually lives there—a little organized clutter usually does the trick.

WHEN YOU WISH UPON A STAR

One of the biggest perks of having a father in the advertising business was that Hockersmith often got to act in the commercials he produced for clients. She fondly recalls one occasion when she choreographed her own little dance to accompany the song "When You Wish Upon a Star." She performed the dance on a local television show while her mother was in the hospital giving birth to Hockersmith's younger sister.

Years later, when she was in Washington, D.C., to decorate the White House, she was relaxing in a restaurant when someone started singing that song. The memory came flooding back, and she was delighted to realize that dreams really can come true.

Museum Curator

WHAT IS A MUSEUM CURATOR?

Rock 'n' roll music, sports, trains, history, cars, fashion, art—all of these industries and interests have museums dedicated solely to them. With about 5,000 museums in the United States, there's something for everyone.

Museums can be run by federal, state, and local governments, nonprofit organizations, colleges, universities, businesses, professional associations, or private citizens. No matter where you find them or what their specialties are, all museums have one thing in common—their need for a curator to put (and keep!) it all together.

Museum curators, sometimes called collections managers, are the experts who develop and oversee the collection of artifacts or other special objects that give the museum its identity: For instance, a curator in a rock 'n' roll museum works with music memorabilia. Depending on the type of museum that they work for, curators might specialize in various types of art, coins, minerals, clothing, maps, animals, plants, or historic sites.

The curator at a typical museum carries many responsibilities, and his or her work involves several stages. First a curator must find and/or acquire interesting and historically significant objects that fit with the overall purpose of the museum. This stage involves a good deal of research and may require some travel to find the right pieces.

Once an object is located, the curator must determine whether the price is reasonable and affordable. Again research is an invaluable tool in this process, because the curator must be certain that the piece is authentic and must be fully aware of its worth in order to do a good job.

Several verbs describe the next stages of a curator's work. Once an object has been obtained—either through a donation or through a purchase—the curator must appraise, insure, analyze, describe, arrange, catalog, restore, preserve, exhibit, maintain, and store it. Some museums have very large staffs, and these duties are divided among them. The curator or another professional takes on the task of arranging the piece in museum exhibits so as to be enjoyed by the museum's visitors. The curator may also help develop various publications and resources to help educate others about the collection. Some curators also spend time actually teaching others about the exhibits.

Finally, curators must keep careful records about each of the items in their collections and go to great lengths to protect each item while it is on display and in storage.

A good education is key to securing a career as a curator. Most curators are highly skilled with advanced degrees. In some of the larger museums, it would be fruitless to apply for a position as a curator without a Ph.D. Fortunately, there are many ways to build your base of experience while learning your way to the top.

Many aspiring curators work at various positions within a museum before assuming the full responsibility of curator. Other museum-related occupations include

administrator, who handles the business side of running a museum in matters such as personnel, budget, and building maintenance. A museum administrator is often in charge of making sure that all the various departments in a museum run smoothly.

archivist, who works with important historical documents, photographs, films, and other information sources. The archivist's job is to find them, organize them, keep records about their origins and whereabouts, and make them available to the people who might need them. Depending on what type of museum or library that an archivist works for, he or she might handle historical documents such as the Declaration of Independence, letters from famous people such as presidents and actors, or special records from important business meetings.

conservator, a highly trained specialist who examines, repairs, and restores art objects. A conservator must be knowledgeable in the science of chemicals and apply what he or she knows about the effects of pollution, the environment, and light on various types of art.

registrar, who acts as a legal guardian for a museum and is in charge of all the paperwork that must be kept about each artifact in the museum. The registrar keeps records that indicate where each piece is located, where it came from, how it is insured, instructions on caring for each piece, and other vital information. A good registrar knows where to find every single piece in the museum's collection at all times—whether it's on display, on loan to another museum, or in storage.

Entry-level positions for people straight out of high school or college might include tour guide, exhibit educator, and gift shop clerk (with more training, gift shop manager or buyer could be an option as well).

There's a lot of work behind the exhibits you see at any museum. The job opportunities in museums are often quite competitive because they can be interesting and fulfilling. Thus, making the challenging quest for a career in this field is well worth the effort.

TRY IT OUT

GET A JOB

Whether for pay or as a volunteer, you can't go wrong by getting involved in your local museum. This experience will let you see firsthand what it takes to run a museum. This involvement will help you know if museum work has a place in your future.

Those of you who decide that you do want a career in this field need to realize that museum experience is considered very important. In fact, most museums won't hire you for the more challenging jobs unless you have a solid track record of other museum work.

CLICK YOUR WAY TO THE WORLD'S MUSEUMS

You don't even have to leave home to tour some of the world's most impressive museums. Many are a step away, in living color, via the Internet. One exceptional website is called Internet ArtResources. It lives up to its claim to be your "complete guide to the visual arts" with more than 6,000 listings about museums and art galleries around the country. The site features six distinctive areas: GalleryWalk, StudioVisit, MuseumStroll, ArtNewStand, ArtShows, and ArtSchools. You'll find answers to many of your questions here. Find it at http://artresources.com.

The Smithsonian also hosts its own gigantic multimedia site. Take a tour of the Air and Space Museum, followed by a visit to the Smithsonian gift shop. You won't want to miss the Museum of African Art or the National Museum of American History. Cap it all off with a visit to the National Zoo. The address to get you started is http://www.si.edu/.

TOUR THE "BIG ONE" ON YOUR PC

The Smithsonian is one of the largest and most well-known museum complexes in the world. Separate museums house extensive collections about space, transportation, natural history, and more. If a trip to Washington, D.C., is not in the near future for you, you can explore the museum on CD-ROM.

Smithsonian's America is a fairly inexpensive resource that can be ordered directly from its publisher, Creative Multimedia, by calling 503-241-4351 or from Egghead Software by calling 800-EGG-HEAD.

BECOME A CRITIC

Visit a local museum—it doesn't matter what kind. Take a notebook and pencil with you, and plan on staying for a while. Gather the available written materials about the exhibit. Read them carefully to get a better idea of what the exhibit is all about. Then take a slow and observant tour of the exhibit. When you are finished, write down your overall impression of the exhibit. Was it interesting? Did it make sense? Could you move from one display to another relatively easily?

Now, take another walk through the exhibit. This time, list each displayed item in your notebook. Make a checklist and note the following:

- ☀ Is it obvious why the object is included in this particular exhibit? Does it belong? Is the description interesting?
- ☀ Can I understand what they are trying to teach me?
- ☀ Do I now know more about the exhibit subject than when I arrived?

PLAN YOUR OWN EXHIBIT

Talk to your school principal or religious leader about your interest in becoming a museum curator. Explain that you'd like the opportunity to test your skills and ask for help in putting together an exhibit about the history of your school or place of worship. Some of the things you might look for are old photographs of the building and its principals, teachers, and students; newspapers clippings about major events such as sports championships; old yearbooks; and maybe even an old sports or band uniform. Talk to as many people as you can about the early days. If your school is too new for this idea, try your church or temple.

Once you've gathered all your materials and received permission to display them, practice arranging them in different ways to get an interesting, visually attractive exhibit that will make sense to viewers. You'll want to write a description of each item and attach it so that viewers can fully understand its significance.

If you find it difficult to find actual artifacts to display, you might want to write a chronology of events from the beginning to the present. You can list these events on posters or in a special booklet.

CHECK IT OUT

American Association of Museums
1225 I Street NW, Suite 200
Washington, D.C. 20005

American Institute for
  Conservation of Historic
  and Artistic Works
1400 16th Street NW, Suite 340
Washington, D.C. 20036

Association of Systematic
  Collections
730 11th Street NW, Second Floor
Washington, D.C. 20001

Society of American Archivists
600 Federal Street, Suite 504
Chicago, Illinois 60605

GET ACQUAINTED

Barbara Luck, Museum Curator

CAREER PATH

CHILDHOOD ASPIRATION: To use art, without being a teacher in the school system.

FIRST JOB: Museum registrar.

CURRENT JOB: Curator of paintings and drawings at the Colonial Williamsburg Foundation.

IT'S LIKE WORKING A GIGANTIC JIGSAW PUZZLE

Barbara Luck is responsible for the paintings and drawings—historical and contemporary—at Colonial Williamsburg. When she acquires a new piece of art, she does a careful study to track its history. Some of the questions she tries to answer are Who made it? Who used it? How was it used? And what did it mean to its owners? This research process can involve digging through volumes of old records and traveling to numerous places to talk to town historians and librarians. She looks for historic documentation as well as personal stories so that each piece comes alive with meaning to the people who visit the museum.

DOES IT PASS THE LUCK TEST?

Through the years, Luck has gained a keen sense of the type of artwork needed to round out the museum collection. Before acquiring something new, each piece must pass Luck's five point test:

- Is this piece authentic?
- Does the museum need this piece?
- Can the museum afford this piece (or will someone donate it for free)?
- Can this piece be transported to the museum and displayed at the museum without being damaged?
- Is this piece unusual, important, significant historically, and aesthetically pleasing?

BIGGEST CHALLENGE

Luck finds challenge and great delight in making 18th-, 19th-, and 20th-century materials relevant to today. She enjoys helping museum visitors of all ages relate what they see in the museum to their own lives.

ADVICE TO FUTURE MUSEUM CURATORS

Luck has these suggestions for aspiring curators.

1. Learn to respond visually to things around you.
2. Practice describing these things so that they make sense and interest others.
3. Get a good education in a field that interests you, but be prepared to learn a lot about this profession on the job.

Photojournalist

WHAT IS A PHOTOJOURNALIST?

The first man on the moon. The space shuttle *Challenger* explosion. The Oklahoma City bombing. Do any of those statements immediately evoke a vivid image in your mind? If so, it's probably because of a photojournalist.

Using both photography and journalism, photojournalists combine the two disciplines to tell compelling stories with pictures. They take pictures of newsworthy events, places, and people for newspapers, magazines, or television shows. They often specialize in a particular kind of photography such as news, sports, social issues, or human interest stories. Some photojournalists focus on covering wars and international events.

Photojournalists can either be employed by a specific newspaper, news show, or magazine, or they can work on freelance assignments. Freelance means that you are self-employed. You work on special projects for a specific client, or you come up with your own ideas for photo essays and sell them to the appropriate media.

Photojournalists must be as familiar with current events and human nature as they are with photographic style and lighting techniques. Their job is to capture the mood and news of our world with a click of their camera shutter.

Related professions range from being a photographic supplier, working in the business of selling "tools" such as cameras, film, and processing equipment, to being a filmmaker,

creating motion pictures
for worldwide audiences. In between these two extremes are
many other opportunities. Commercial photographers work in
areas that include advertising, public relations, and marketing.
Studio photographers take pictures that mark important events
in people's lives—baby's first picture, senior portraits, and the
like. Photographers who specialize in the educational field may
teach, produce audiovisual aids and training films, or provide
appropriate pictures to illustrate textbooks.

There is quite a variety of training options for someone interested in a photography career. How much training you'll need
depends on what you intend to do. For some jobs, high school
photography courses provide all the training you need to get
started. Others require a two- or four-year degree with a major in
photography. A degree with some combination of photography
and journalism would be useful for an aspiring photojournalist.

Learning from an expert through an apprenticeship is yet
another option. If completed in a portrait or commercial studio,
an apprenticeship could provide training in more than one
aspect of photography, including processing film and lighting
techniques.

Perhaps one of the most exciting aspects of photography is
its potential to let you earn while you learn. For instance, if
you've successfully completed high school photography training, you might find it possible to work in a studio while earning
a degree in photojournalism.

TRY IT OUT

PHOTOGRAPHER ON THE LOOSE

Family reunions, school assemblies, nature hikes—someone interested in a photography career shouldn't be caught at events like these without a camera. Practice makes perfect when it comes to photography. Every time you develop a roll of film, you'll learn how to improve your technique.

Make sure you submit those especially good shots to your community or school newspaper. Every picture that gets published is another page for your photography portfolio. Future employers will be impressed that you had the courage and talent to get published as a teenager.

JOIN THE CLUB

If the idea of becoming a photographer is pretty new to you, you'll have to start with the basics. Joining The Activities Club is one way to get started. The club's Photography in a Snap program teaches the art of photography and includes a 35-mm camera, film, a coupon for free film developing, a Do Not Disturb sign, and activity cards that describe how to mount and frame a photo and create a family picture tree. The kit can be ordered by calling 800-873-5487 or writing The Activities Club, 59 Rosedale Road, Watertown, Massachusetts 02172.

MAKE A PHOTO SCRAPBOOK

You don't have to go any farther than your local supermarket or bookstore to find exceptional examples of photojournalism. Pick up copies of magazines such as *Life*, *National Geographic*, or *Sports Illustrated* and look for pictures that thrill and inspire. Clip these photos and paste them in a special notebook. Keep notes on where you found the photo, the photographer, and what you like about the photograph. It won't be long before you can start adding your own photos to the scrapbook!

STRAIGHT TO THE SOURCE

Eastman Kodak (the company famous for its film) has quite an array of information on the Internet. Visit the company on-line at http://www.kodak.com.

The company also produces and provides to the general public a number of useful educational resources, such as its free publication *Photography in Your Future* (publication #AT-15). To request a copy, call Eastman Kodak at 800-242-2424.

THE PHOTOGRAPHY PAGE

While you are on-line, make sure to stop by the Photography Page at http://www.mcs.net/~rjacobs/home.html. This site includes all sorts of information about techniques, equipment, contests, and reviews of photo-related publications. It also provides links to other photography hot spots on the Web, so you can explore home pages for organizations such as the Photographic Society of America and the North American Nature Photography Association.

Yet another popular website for photojournalists is found at http://www.tangointeractive.com. This one is actually run by an experienced photojournalist.

CHECK IT OUT

National Press Photographers Association
3200 Crowsdale, Suite 306
Durham, North Carolina 27705

North American Nature Photography Association
10200 West 44th Avenue, Suite 304
Wheat Ridge, Colorado 80033-2840

Professional Photographers of America
1090 Executive Way
Des Plaines, Illinois 60018

GET ACQUAINTED

Stephen Shames,
Freelance Photojournalist

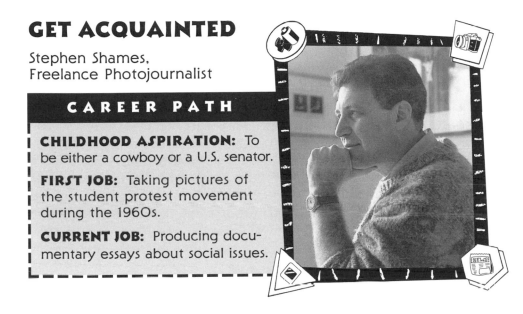

CAREER PATH

CHILDHOOD ASPIRATION: To be either a cowboy or a U.S. senator.

FIRST JOB: Taking pictures of the student protest movement during the 1960s.

CURRENT JOB: Producing documentary essays about social issues.

Stephen Shames accidentally found his career as a photojournalist when he was a history major at the University of California-Berkeley. He took a photography class at the student union, discovered that he was good at it, and concluded that it was more fun to earn his way through college taking pictures than washing dishes.

By the time he graduated, he had established himself as a credible photojournalist by covering the protest movement of the 1960s (ask your parents or teachers about groups such as the Black Panther Party, People's Park, and Angela Davis). When he left college, he worked as a freelance photojournalist for publications such as *Newsweek*, the *New York Times*, and *Time*.

PLACES TO LOOK FOR SHAMES' WORK

You can find Shames' work on the front page of a national newspaper, in national news magazines such as *Time* and *Newsweek*, on a television news program, in a school textbook, in an art museum exhibit, or in one of Shames' photo essay books—*Outside the Dream: Children in Poverty in America* (New York: Aperture, 1991) or *Pursuing the Dream:*

What Helps Children and Their Families Succeed (New York: Aperture, 1997).

THE PHOTOJOURNALIST AS AN ARTIST

Like other artists, professional photojournalists learn how to express their feelings through their art. Shames says that it takes a lifetime to move from taking pictures to producing art with a camera. Unlike other artists, photojournalists often have just a split second to create their art. Everything a photojournalist has learned about photography, people, and history has to come together in a flash to record the truly great moments in history.

BEYOND THE STARVING ARTIST MYTH

Freelance photojournalism is a competitive business. The people who treat it as a business are the ones who are most likely to make a good living at it.

One secret to success is making multiple sales from one project. For example, Shames once spent five months riding along in a squad car with the Houston homicide police. He took pictures of them as they answered calls, investigated cases, and interrogated suspects. Shames sold pictures from that project to a regional magazine, a national news magazine, a television news show, an encyclopedia publisher, and a textbook publisher. He used one of the photos in his own book on children in poverty. Some of the pictures were also featured in a six-page essay on domestic violence as part of a *Newsweek* story on the O.J. Simpson trial.

Shames is affiliated with Matrix, an international photo agency. They help him sell his photographs, including the homicide work.

SNAP TO IT

Photojournalists have to go to the news; they can't wait for news to come to them. This means keeping their bags packed and being ready to travel anywhere in the world on a moment's notice. Shames says that it's not unusual for a photojournalist to be on the road from 100 to 200 days a year.

YOU HEARD IT HERE FIRST

The industry is changing and will belong to those who can keep up with the change. Digital cameras and other high-tech equipment will redefine the industry within the next few years. One thing that will never change is that photojournalists will still be storytellers. No matter what the technology, the pictures will continue to be the key.

ADVICE TO FUTURE PHOTOJOURNALISTS

Think, stay ahead of the game, and learn to make your own opportunities.

MAKE AN ARTISTIC DETOUR!

Go ahead. Feel free to dismiss completely the notion of the starving artist. Once you realize that the range of artistic career opportunities can include a full range of creative endeavors, you'll find about 1.3 million jobs per year in a $314 billion business.

That's big, so big, in fact, that some people estimate that one in three children will be employed in an arts-related occupation someday. That means many opportunities for the artistically inclined. If you don't believe it, just check out the following artistic ideas. For more information on what these jobs entail try looking them up in career encyclopedias (see list on page 160).

A WORLD OF ARTISTIC CAREERS

SHARE YOUR TALENT

Many who've been blessed with artistic talents of one kind or another have found great satisfaction in educating others. This route often provides the means of making art the focal point of a career while also providing a regular paycheck and opportunities for career advancement.

art education
  curriculum writer
art historian
art librarian
art teacher
choir director
dance teacher

dance therapist
docent
museum educator
music libararian
musicologist
music therapist
piano teacher

school arts
  coordinator
speech teacher
speech therapist
theater teacher
vocal teacher

MAKE ART YOUR BUSINESS

Does it surprise you to discover that the business world is one of the best places to put your artistic talents to work? There are many ways to blend your artistic bent with the creative needs of business. A few ideas to consider include

advertising artist
apparel engineer
art director
  (advertising,
  publishing, etc.)
arts marketer
automobile designer
billboard artist
book illustrator
calligrapher
caricaturist
cartographer
clothing designer
color specialist
computer graphics
  designer
display designer
draftsperson

equipment designer
exhibit designer
fabric designer
fashion cutter
floral designer
furniture designer
graphic designer
greeting card
  illustrator
holographer
industrial designer
instrument manu-
  facturer
interior designer
knitting designer
layout artist
leather goods designer
lithographer

machinery designer
milliner
mold maker
music engraver
neon sign maker
newspaper illustrator
optical effects
  engineer
ornament designer
package designer
paper maker
parade float designer
pattern designer
product designer
record cover designer
retail buyer
shoe designer
software designer

sound effects
  technician
tattoo artist
textile designer

theme park designer
tile designer
toy designer
typographer

upholsterer
wallpaper designer
window designer
yarn dyer

NO MORE STARVING ARTISTS

If creating art in its purest and simplest form is what you want to do, here are some creative outlets to consider. Just remember, making it and selling it are two different things. Find a way to make it pay!

basket maker
bead maker
china painter/
  designer
engraver
framer
glassblower
handicrafter
ice sculptor

instrument designer/
  builder/repairer
jewelry designer
kinetic artist
knitter
lacemaker
muralist
needleworker
painter

photographer
potter
printmaker
sculptor
serigrapher
stained glass artist
tapestry artist
weaver
woodworker
xylographer

A POTPOURRI OF CREATIVE CAREER IDEAS

Put some creative thought into using your artistic talent in some unusual and even unexpected ways. Here are some ideas to get you thinking.

aerial photographer
aeronautical designer
anatomical
  diagrammer
archaeologist
architectural
  model builder
art appraiser
art conservator
arts and entertain-
  ment journalist
arts attorney
artist's agent
auctioneer

booking agent
contract specialist
copyright specialist
critic
environmental
  designer
facility planner
fund-raiser (devel-
  opment director)
gallery owner/
  salesperson
glaze technologist
golf course designer
landscape architect

makeup artist
museum curator
music contractor
music editor
nightclub manager
photojournalist
piano tuner
police artist
program director
  (TV, radio, arts
  organizations, etc.)
ticketing agent
urban planner
writer

THE ROAR OF APPLAUSE

If you are an artist who can't resist the thrill of an encore performance, consider some of these career ideas that put you (or your work) in the spotlight.

accompanist
actor
announcer
art festival coordinator
artistic director
  (theater, film)
audio engineer
ballet dancer
band director
box office manager
artist's agent
casting director
choreographer
cinematographer
clown
comedian
composer
concert promoter
concert musician
concert singer
conductor
costume buyer

costume designer
cruise ship enter-
  tainment director
dancer
disc jockey
documentary
  producer
electric/acoustical
  engineer
keyboard technician
film editor
filmmaker
gaffer
instrumentalist
lyricist
magician
mime
motion picture
  animator
music publisher
news anchorperson
orchestrator

playwright
producer (TV, radio,
  theater, movies)
props designer
recording engineer
  and mixer
record producer
rigger
scene painter
screenwriter/
  scriptwriter
set designer
songwriter
sound engineer
stagehand
theater director
TV camera operator
videographer
vocalist
voice-over artist
wardrobe mistress/
  manager

KEEP IN MIND

Here are a couple of things to keep in mind as you continue to ponder the artistic possibilities.

Mix and Match Your Skills

Anything you can do in another field, you can do in the arts; for example, if you love math and the arts, think about becoming an accountant for an arts organization or museum. If you love all things technical and the arts, think about blending the two as a sound or lighting technician, a CD-ROM designer, or a sound mixer. If arts and writing are your top two, think about a career as an arts reporter, a public relations specialist for an arts organization, or a development officer.

Whatever your unique blend of skills and interests may be, there's a creative way to mix and match them in an arts-related profession.

The Art of Show and Tell

Perhaps more than any other professional field, the art world relies on show and tell. Many of these professions are visually oriented. You can talk about painting a great picture, but you'll make more impact (and more commissions) if you can prove it.

That's why a portfolio is so important for artists of all kinds. A portfolio provides an orderly, visually attractive "résumé" of your work. It includes samples of your best work to showcase your personal style and achievements for prospective employers and clients. It's never too early to get into the portfolio habit. Start compiling your best work now.

INFORMATION IS POWER

Mind-boggling, isn't it? There are so many great choices, so many jobs you've never heard of before. How will you ever narrow it down to the perfect spot for you?

First, pinpoint the ideas that sound the most interesting to you. Then, find out all you can about them. As you may have noticed, a similar pattern of information was used for each of the career entries featured in this book. Each entry included

- ☼ a general description or definition of the career
- ☼ some hands-on projects that give readers a chance to actually experience a job
- ☼ a list of organizations to contact for more information
- ☼ an interview with a professional

You can use information like this to help you determine the best career path to pursue. Since there isn't room in one book to profile all arts-related career choices, here's your chance to do it yourself. Conduct a full investigation into an art career that interests you.

Please Note: If this book does not belong to you use a separate sheet of paper to record your responses to the following questions.

CAREER TITLE _____

WHAT IS A _____?
Use career encyclopedias and other resources to write a description of this career.

_____
_____
_____

```
SKILL SET
✔ _____
✔ _____
✔ _____
```

TRY IT OUT
Write project ideas here. Ask your parents and your teacher to come up with a plan.

_____
_____
_____

CHECK IT OUT
List professional organizations where you can learn more about this profession.

_____
_____
_____

GET ACQUAINTED
Interview a professional in the field and summarize your findings.

_____
_____
_____

DON'T STOP NOW!
GO FOR IT!

It's been a fast-paced trip so far. Take a break, regroup, and look at all the progress you've made.

1st Stop: Self-Discovery
You discovered some personal interests and natural abilities that you can start building a career around.

2nd Stop: Exploration
You've explored an exciting array of career opportunities in science. You're now aware that your career can involve either a heavy-duty dose of science and all the educational requirements it may involve or that it can involve a practical application of scientific methods with a minimum of training and experience.

   At this point, you've found a couple (or few) careers that really intrigue you. Now it's time to put it all together and do all you can to make an informed, intelligent choice. It's time to move on to the

3rd Stop: Experimentation

By the time you finish this section, you'll have reached one of three points in the career planning process.

1. **Green light!** You found it. No need to look any further. This is *the* career for you. (This may happen to a lucky few. Don't worry if it hasn't happened yet for you. This whole process is about exploring options, experimenting with ideas, and, eventually, making the best choice for you.)

2. **Yellow light!** Close, but not quite. You seem to be on the right path but you haven't nailed things down for sure. (This is where many people your age end up, and it's a good place to be. You've learned what it takes to really check things out. Hang in there. Your time will come.

3. **Red light!** Whoa! No doubt about it, this career just isn't for you. (Congratulations! Aren't you glad you found out now and not after you'd spent four years in college preparing for this career? Your next stop: Make a U-turn and start this process over with another career.)

Here's a sneak peek at what you'll be doing in the next section.

☼ First, you'll pick a favorite career idea (or two or three).
☼ Second, you'll snoop around the library to find answers to the 10 things you've just got to know about your future career.
☼ Third, you'll pick up the phone and talk to someone whose career you admire to find out what it's really like.
☼ Fourth, you'll link up with a whole world of great information about your career idea on the Internet (it's easier than you think).
☼ Fifth, you'll go on the job to shadow a professional for a day.

Hang on to your hats and get ready to make tracks!

#1 NARROW DOWN YOUR CHOICES

You've been introduced to quite a few art career ideas. You may also have some ideas of your own to add. Which ones appeal to you the most?

Write your top three choices in the spaces below. (Sorry if this is starting to sound like a broken record, but . . . if this book does not belong to you, write your responses on a separate sheet of paper.)

1. _____
2. _____
3. _____

#2 SNOOP AT THE LIBRARY

Take your list of favorite career ideas, a notebook, and a helpful adult with you to the library. When you get there, go to the reference section and ask the librarian to help you find

books about careers. Most libraries will have at least one set of career encyclopedias. Some of the larger libraries may also have career information on CD-ROM.

Gather all the information you can and use it to answer the following questions in your notebook about each of the careers on your list. Make sure to ask for help if you get stuck.

TOP 10 THINGS YOU NEED TO KNOW ABOUT YOUR CAREER

1. What kinds of skills does this job require?
2. What kind of training is required? (Compare the options for a high school degree, trade school degree, two-year degree, four-year degree, and advanced degree.)
3. What types of classes do I need to take in high school in order to be accepted into a training program?
4. What are the names of three schools or colleges where I can get the training I need?
5. Are there any apprenticeship or internship opportunities available? If so, where? If not, could I create my own opportunity? How?
6. How much money can I expect to earn as a beginner? How much with more experience?
7. What kinds of places hire people to do this kind of work?
8. What is a typical work environment like? For example, would I work in a busy office, outdoors, or in a laboratory?
9. What are some books and magazines I could read to learn more about this career? Make a list and look for them at your library.
10. Where can I write for more information? Make a list of professional associations.

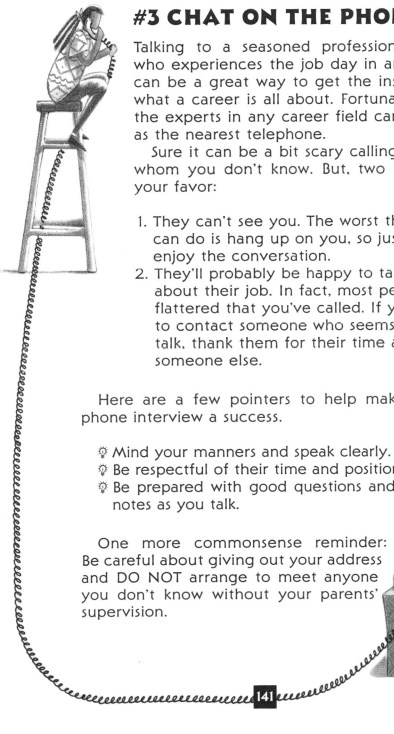

#3 CHAT ON THE PHONE

Talking to a seasoned professional—someone who experiences the job day in and day out—can be a great way to get the inside story on what a career is all about. Fortunately for you, the experts in any career field can be as close as the nearest telephone.

Sure it can be a bit scary calling up an adult whom you don't know. But, two things are in your favor:

1. They can't see you. The worst thing they can do is hang up on you, so just relax and enjoy the conversation.
2. They'll probably be happy to talk to you about their job. In fact, most people will be flattered that you've called. If you happen to contact someone who seems reluctant to talk, thank them for their time and try someone else.

Here are a few pointers to help make your telephone interview a success.

- ☼ Mind your manners and speak clearly.
- ☼ Be respectful of their time and position.
- ☼ Be prepared with good questions and take notes as you talk.

One more commonsense reminder: Be careful about giving out your address and DO NOT arrange to meet anyone you don't know without your parents' supervision.

TRACKING DOWN CAREER EXPERTS

You might be wondering by now how to find someone to interview. Have no fear! It's easy, if you're persistent. All you have to do is ask. Ask the right people and you'll have a great lead in no time.

A few of the people to ask and sources to turn to are

Your parents. They may know someone (or know someone who knows someone) who has just the kind of job you're looking for.

Your friends and neighbors. You might be surprised to find out how many interesting jobs these people have when you start asking them what they (or their parents) do for a living.

Librarians. Since you've already figured out what kinds of companies employ people in your field of interest, the next step is to ask for information about local employers. Although it's a bit cumbersome to use, a big volume called *Contacts Influential* can provide this kind of information.

Professional associations. Call or write to the professional associations you discovered in Activity #1 a few pages back and ask for recommendations.

Chambers of commerce. The local chamber of commerce probably has a directory of employers, their specialties, and their phone numbers. Call the chamber, explain what you are looking for, and give the person a chance to help the future workforce.

Newspaper and magazine articles. Find an article about the subject you are interested in. Chances are pretty good that it will mention the name of at least one expert in the field. The article probably won't include the person's phone number (that would be too easy), so you'll have to look for clues. Common clues include the name of the company that the expert works for, the town that he or she lives in, and if the person is an author, the name of his or her publisher. Make a few phone calls and track the person down (if long distance calls are involved, make sure to get your parents' permission first).

INQUIRING KIDS WANT TO KNOW

Before you make the call, make a list of questions to ask. You'll cover more ground if you focus on using the five w's (and the h) that you've probably heard about in your creative writing classes: Who? What? Where? When? How? and Why? For example,

1. Who do you work for?
2. What is a typical work day like for you?
3. Where can I get some on-the-job experience?
4. When did you become a _____ ?
   (profession)
5. How much can you earn in this profession? (But, remember it's not polite to ask someone how much *he* or *she* earns.)
6. Why did you choose this profession?

One last suggestion: Add a professional (and very classy) touch to the interview process by following up with a thank-you note to the person who took time out of a busy schedule to talk with you.

#4 SURF THE NET

With the Internet, the new information super-highway, charging full steam ahead, you literally have a world of information at your fingertips. The Internet has something for everyone, and it's getting easier to access all the time. An increasing number of libraries and schools are

offering access to the Internet on their computers. In addition, companies such as America Online and CompuServe have made it possible for anyone with a home computer to surf the World Wide Web.

A typical career search will land everything from the latest news on developments in the field and course notes from universities to museum exhibits, interactive games, educational activities, and more. You just can't beat the timeliness or the variety of information available on the Net.

One of the easiest ways to track down this information is to use an Internet search engine, such as Yahoo! Simply type in the topic you are looking for, and in a matter of seconds, you'll have a list of options from around the world. It's fun to browse—you never know what you'll come up with.

To narrow down your search a bit, look for specific websites, forums, or chatrooms that are related to your topic in the following publications:

Hahn, Harley. *The Internet Yellow Pages.* Berkeley, Calif.: Osborne McGraw Hill, 1997.

———. *The World Wide Web Yellow Pages.* Berkeley, Calif.: Osborne McGraw Hill, 1997.

To go on-line at home you may want to compare two of the more popular on-line services: America Online and CompuServe. Please note that there is a monthly subscription fee for using these services. There can also be extra fees attached to specific forums and services, so *make sure you have your parents' OK before you sign up.* For information about America Online call 800-827-6364. For information about CompuServe call 800-848-8990. Both services frequently offer free start-up deals, so shop around.

There are also many other services, depending on where you live. Check your local phone book or ads in local computer magazines for other service options.

Before you link up, keep in mind that many of these sites are geared toward professionals who are already working in a particular field. Some of the sites can get pretty technical. Just use the experience as a chance to nose around the field, hang out with the people who are tops in the field, and think about whether or not you'd like to be involved in a profession like that.

Specific sites to look for are the following:

Professional associations. Find out about what's happening in the field, conferences, journals, and other helpful tidbits.

Schools that specialize in this area. Many include research tools, introductory courses, and all kinds of interesting information.

Government agencies. Quite a few are going high-tech with lots of helpful resources.

Websites hosted by experts in the field (this seems to be a popular hobby among many professionals). These websites are often as entertaining as they are informative.

If you're not sure where to go, just start clicking around. Sites often link to other sites. You may want to jot down notes about favorite sites. Sometimes you can even print out information that isn't copyright-protected; try the print option and see what happens.

Be prepared: Surfing the Internet can be an addicting habit! There is so much awesome information. It's a fun way to focus on your future.

#5 SHADOW A PROFESSIONAL

Linking up with someone who is gainfully employed in a profession that you want to explore is a great way to find out what a career is like. Following someone around while the person is at work is called "shadowing." Try it!

This process involves three steps.

1. Find someone to shadow. Some suggestions include
   - ☼ the person you interviewed (if you enjoyed talking with him or her and feel comfortable about asking the person to show you around his or her workplace)
   - ☼ friends and neighbors (you may even be shocked to discover that your parents have interesting jobs)
   - ☼ workers at the chamber of commerce may know of mentoring programs available in your area (it's a popular concept, so most larger areas should have something going on)
   - ☼ someone at your local School-to-Work office, the local Boy Scouts Explorer program director (this is available to girls too!), or your school guidance counselor
2. Make a date. Call and make an appointment. Find out when is the best time for arrival and departure. Make arrangements with a parent or other respected adult to go with you and get there on time.
3. Keep your ears and eyes open. This is one time when it is OK to be nosy. Ask questions. Notice everything that is happening around you. Ask your host to let you try some of the tasks he or she is doing.

The basic idea of the shadowing experience is to put yourself in the other person's shoes and see how they fit. Imagine yourself having a job like this 10 or 15 years down the road. It's a great way to find out if you are suited for a particular line of work.

BE CAREFUL OUT THERE!

Two cautions must accompany this recommendation. First, remember the stranger danger rules of your childhood. NEVER meet with anyone you don't know without your parents' permission and ALWAYS meet in a supervised situation—at the office or with your parents.

Second, be careful not to overdo it. These people are busy earning a living, so respect their time by limiting your contact and coming prepared with valid questions and background information.

PLAN B

If shadowing opportunities are limited where you live, try one of these approaches for learning the ropes from a professional.

Pen pals. Find a mentor who is willing to share information, send interesting materials, or answer specific questions that come up during your search.

Cyber pals. Go on-line in a forum or chatroom related to your profession. You'll be able to chat with professionals from all over the world.

If you want to get some more on-the-job experience, try one of these approaches.

Volunteer to do the dirty work. Volunteer to work for someone who has a job that interests you for a specified period of time. Do anything—filing, errands, emptying trash cans—that puts you in contact with professionals. Notice every tiny detail about the profession. Listen to the lingo they use in the profession. Watch how they perform their jobs on a day-to-day basis.

Be an apprentice. This centuries-old job training method is making a comeback. Find out if you can set up an official on-the-job training program to gain valuable experience.

Ask professional associations about apprenticeship opportunities. Once again, a School-to-Work program can be a great asset. In many areas, they've established some very interesting career training opportunities.

Hire yourself for the job. Maybe you are simply too young to do much in the way of on-the-job training right now. That's OK. Start learning all you can now and you'll be ready to really wow them when the time is right. Make sure you do all the Try It Out activities included for the career(s) you are most interested in. Use those activities as a starting point for creating other projects that will give you a feel for what the job is like.

WHAT'S NEXT?

Have you carefully worked your way through all of the suggested activities? You haven't tried to sneak past anything, have you? This isn't a place for shortcuts. If you've done the activities, you're ready to decide where you stand with each career idea. So what is it? Green light? See page 152. Yellow light? See page 151. Red light? See page 150. Find the spot that best describes your response to what you've discovered about this career idea and plan your next move.

RED LIGHT

So you've decided this career is definitely not for you—hang in there! The process of elimination is an important one. You've learned some valuable career planning skills; use them to explore other ideas. In the meantime, use the following road map to chart a plan to get beyond this "spinning your wheels" point in the process.

Take a variety of classes at school to expose yourself to new ideas and expand the options. Make a list of courses you want to try.

- ☼ _____
- ☼ _____
- ☼ _____
- ☼ _____

Get involved in clubs and other after-school activities (like 4-H or Boy Scout Explorers) to further develop your interests. Write down some that interest you.

- ☼ _____
- ☼ _____
- ☼ _____
- ☼ _____

Read all you can find about interesting people and their work. Make a list of people you'd like to learn more about.

- ☼ _____
- ☼ _____
- ☼ _____
- ☼ _____

Keep at it. Time is on your side. Finding the perfect work for you is worth a little effort. Once you've crossed this hurdle, move on to the next pages and continue mapping out a great future.

YELLOW LIGHT

Proceed with caution. While the idea continues to intrigue you, you may wonder if it's the best choice for you. Your concerns are legitimate (listen to that nagging little voice inside!).

Maybe it's the training requirements that intimidate you. Maybe you have concerns about finding a good job once you complete the training. Maybe you wonder if you have what it takes to do the job.

At this point, it's good to remember that there is often more than one way to get somewhere. Check out all the choices and choose the route that's best for you. Use the following road map to move on down the road in your career planning adventure.

Make two lists. On the first, list the things you like most about the career you are currently investigating. On the second, list the things that are most important to you in a future career. Look for similarities on both lists and focus on careers that emphasize these similar key points.

Current Career	Future Career
☼ _____	☼ _____
☼ _____	☼ _____

What are some career ideas that are similar to the one you have in mind? Find out all you can about them. Go back through the exploration process explained on pages 139 to 148 and repeat some of the exercises that were most valuable.

☼ _____

☼ _____

☼ _____

☼ _____

Visit your school counselor and ask him or her which career assessment tools are available through your school. Use these to find out more about your strengths and interests. List the date, time, and place for any assessment tests you plan to take.

- ☼ _____
- ☼ _____
- ☼ _____
- ☼ _____

What other adults do you know and respect to whom you can talk about your future? They may have ideas that you've never thought of.

- ☼ _____
- ☼ _____
- ☼ _____
- ☼ _____

What kinds of part-time jobs, volunteer work, or after-school experiences can you look into that will give you a chance to build your skills and test your abilities? Think about how you can tap into these opportunities.

- ☼ _____
- ☼ _____
- ☼ _____
- ☼ _____

GREEN LIGHT

Yahoo! You are totally turned on to this career idea and ready to do whatever it takes to make it your life's work. Go for it!

Find out what kinds of classes you need to take now to prepare for this career. List them here.

- ☼ _____
- ☼ _____
- ☼ _____
- ☼ _____

What are some on-the-job training possibilities for you to pursue? List the company name, a person to contact and the phone number.

- 💡 _____
- 💡 _____
- 💡 _____
- 💡 _____

Find out if there are any internship or apprenticeship opportunities available in this career field. List contacts and phone numbers.

- 💡 _____
- 💡 _____
- 💡 _____
- 💡 _____

What kind of education will you need after you graduate from high school? Describe the options.

- 💡 _____
- 💡 _____
- 💡 _____
- 💡 _____

No matter what the educational requirements are, the better your grades are during junior and senior high school, the better your chances for the future.

Take a minute to think about some areas that need improvement in your schoolwork. Write your goals for giving it all you've got here.

- 💡 _____
- 💡 _____
- 💡 _____
- 💡 _____

Where can you get the training you'll need? Make a list of colleges, technical schools, or vocational programs. Include addresses so that you can write to request a catalog.

🔆 _____

🔆 _____

🔆 _____

🔆 _____

HOORAY! YOU DID IT!

This has been quite a trip. If someone tries to tell you that this process is easy, don't believe it. Figuring out what you want to do with the rest of your life is heavy stuff, and it should be. If you don't put some thought (and some sweat and hard work) into the process, you'll get stuck with whatever comes your way.

You may not have things planned to a T. Actually, it's probably better if you don't. You'll change some of your ideas as you grow and experience new things. And, you may find an interesting detour or two along the way. That's OK.

The most important thing about beginning this process now is that you've started to dream. You've discovered that you have some unique talents and abilities to share. You've become aware of some of the ways you can use them to make a living—and, perhaps, make a difference in the world.

Whatever you do, don't lose sight of the hopes and dreams you've discovered. You've got your entire future ahead of you. Use it wisely.

SOME FUTURE DESTINATIONS

Wow! You've really made tracks during this whole process. Now that you've gotten this far, you'll want to keep moving forward to a great future. This section will point you toward some useful resources to help you make a conscientious career choice (that's just the opposite of falling into any old job on a fluke).

IT'S NOT JUST FOR NERDS

The school counselor's office is not just a place where teachers send troublemakers. One of its main purposes is to help students like you make the most of your educational opportunities. Most schools will have a number of useful resources, including career assessment tools (ask about the Self-Directed Search Career Explorer or the COPS Interest Inventory—these are especially useful assessments for people your age). There may also be a stash of books, videos, and other helpful materials.

Make sure no one's looking and sneak into your school counseling office to get some expert advice!

AWESOME INTERNET CAREER RESOURCES

Your parents will be green with envy when they see all the career planning resources you have at your fingertips. Get ready to hear them whine, "But they didn't have all this stuff when I was a kid." Make the most of these cyberspace opportunities.

- ☼ The Career Center for Teens (a site sponsored by Public Television Outreach) includes activities and information on 21st-century career opportunities. Find it at http://www.pbs.org/jobs/teenindex.html.
- ☼ Future Scan includes in-depth profiles on a wide variety of career choices and expert advice from their "Guidance Gurus." Check it out at http://www.future-scan.com.
- ☼ Just for fun visit the Jam!z Knowzone Careers page and chat with other kids about your career dreams. You'll find them by going to http://www.jamz.com and then clicking on the KnowZone icon. (Behave yourself; it's monitored!)
- ☼ JobSmart's Career Guides is another site to explore specific career choices. Look for it at http://www.job-smart.org/tools/career/spec-car.htm.

IT'S NOT JUST FOR BOYS

Boys and girls alike are encouraged to contact their local version of the Boy Scouts Explorer program. It offers exciting on-the-job training experiences in a variety of professional fields. Look in the white pages of your community phone book for the local Boy Scouts of America program.

MORE CAREER BOOKS ESPECIALLY FOR THE ARTISTICALLY INCLINED

Art is a field that offers more opportunity than a single book can contain. Keep looking for the perfect fit for your artistic ambitions. Start with some of the following books.

Bradstein, Eve, and Joanna Lipari. *The Actor: A Practical Guide to a Professional Career.* New York: Donald I. Fine, 1987.

Buzzell, Lida. *How to Make It in Hollywood.* New York: HarperCollins, 1992.

Career Choices for Students of Art. New York: Walker and Co., 1990.

Cohen, Lilly, and Dennis Young. *Careers for Dreamers & Doers: A Guide to Management in the Nonprofit Sector.* New York: The Foundation Center, 1989.

Field, Shelly. *Career Opportunities in Theater and the Performing Arts.* New York: Facts On File, 1992.

————. *Career Opportunities in the Music Industry.* New York: Facts On File, 1990.

————. *100 Best Careers in Entertainment: Discover the Exciting Job Opportunities Waiting for You—In the Spotlight and Behind the Scenes!* New York: Macmillan, 1995.

Foote-Smith, Elizabeth. *Opportunities in Writing Careers.* Lincolnwood, Ill.: National Textbook Co., 1989.

Gibson, James. *Playing for Pay: How to Be a Working Musician.* Cincinnati: Writer's Digest Books, 1990.

Goldfab, Roz. *Careers by Design: A Headhunter's Secrets for Success and Survival in Graphic Design.* New York: Allworth Press, 1993.

Grant, Daniel. *On Becoming an Artist.* New York: Allworth Press, 1993.

Guiley, Rosemary Ellen. *Career Opportunities for Writers.* New York: Facts On File, 1993.

Haubenstock, Susan H., and David Joselit. *Career Opportunities in Art.* New York: Facts On File, 1993.

Henry, Mari Lyn, and Lynne Rogers. *How to Be a Working Actor: An Insider's Guide to Finding Jobs in Theater, Film and Television.* New York: M. Evans and Co., 1989.

Hoover, Deborah A. *Supporting Yourself as an Artist.* New York: Oxford University Press, 1989.

Langly, Stephen, and James Abruzzo. *Jobs in Arts and Media Management: What They Are and How to Get One!* New York: American Council for the Arts, 1986.

Lazarus, Paul N. *Working in Film: The Marketplace in the 90's.* New York: St. Martin's Press, 1993.

Matson, Katinka. *The Working Actor: A Guide to the Profession.* New York: Viking Penguin, 1993.

Morgan, Bradley J., and Joseph M. Palmisano. *Performing Arts Career Directory: A Practical, One-Stop Guide to Getting a Job in Performing Arts.* Detroit: Visible Ink Press, 1994.

Riordan, James. *Making It in the New Music Business.* Cincinnati: Writer's Digest Books, 1991.

Siegel, Alan H. *Breaking Into the Music Business.* New York: Simon & Schuster, 1990.

Siskind, Barry. *The Successful Exhibitor's Handbook.* Bellingham, Wash.: Self-Counsel Press, Inc., 1993.

Taylor, Hugh. *The Hollywood Job-Hunter's Survival Guide: An Insider's Winning Strategies to Getting That (All-Important) First Job.* Los Angeles: Lone Eagle Publishing Company, 1993.

Uscher, Nancy. *Your Own Way in Music: A Career and Resource Guide.* New York: St. Martin's Press, 1990.

Weissman, Dick. *The Music Business: Career Opportunities and Self-Defense.* New York: Crown Publishers, 1990.

HEAVY-DUTY RESOURCES

Career encyclopedias provide general information about a lot of professions and can be a great place to start a career search. Those listed here are easy to use and provide useful information about nearly a zillion different jobs. Look for them in the reference section of your local library.

Cosgrove, Holli, ed. *Career Discovery Encyclopedia: 1997 Edition.* Chicago: J. G. Ferguson Publishing Company, 1997.

Encyclopedia of Career Choices for the 1990's. New York: Perigee Books/Putnam Publishing Group, 1992.

Maze, Marilyn, Donald Mayall, and J. Michael Farr. *The Enhanced Guide for Occupational Exploration: Descriptions for the 2,500 Most Important Jobs.* Indianapolis: JIST, 1995.

VGM's Careers Encyclopedia. Lincolnwood, Ill.: VGM Career Books, 1997.

FINDING PLACES TO WORK

Use resources like these to find leads on local businesses, mentors, job shadowing opportunities, and internships. Later, use these same resources to find a great job!

Lathrop, Richard. *Who's Hiring Who?* Berkeley, Calif.: Ten Speed Press, 1989.

LeCompte, Michelle. *Job Hunter's Sourcebook: Where to Find Employment Leads and Other Job Search Resources.* Detroit: Gale Research Inc., 1996.

Also consult the Job Bank series (Holbrook, Mass.: Adams Media Group). Adams publishes separate guides for Atlanta, Seattle, and many major points in between. Ask your local librarian if they have a guide for the biggest city near you.

FINDING PLACES TO PRACTICE JOB SKILLS

An apprenticeship is an official opportunity to learn a specific profession by working side by side with a skilled professional. As a training method, it's as old as the hills, and it's making a comeback in a big way because people are realizing that doing a job is simply the best way to learn a job.

An internship is an official opportunity to gain work experience (paid or unpaid) in an industry of interest. Interns are more likely to be given entry-level tasks but often have the chance to rub elbows with people in key positions within a company. In comparison to an apprenticeship, which offers very detailed training for a specific job, an internship offers a broader look at a particular kind of work environment.

Both are great ways to learn the ropes and stay one step ahead of the competition. Consider it dress rehearsal for the real thing!

Cantrell, Will. *International Internships and Volunteer Programs.* Oakton, Va.: World Wise Books, 1992.

Guide to Apprenticeship Programs for Non-College Bound Youth. New York: Rosen, 1996.

Hepburn, Diane, ed. *Internships 1997.* Princeton, N.J.: Peterson's, 1997.

Summerfield, Carol J., and Holli Cosgrove. *Ferguson's Guide to Apprenticeship Programs: Traditional and Nontraditional.* Chicago: Ferguson's, 1994.

NO-COLLEGE OCCUPATIONS

Some of you will be relieved to learn that a college degree is not the only route to a satisfying, well-paying career. Whew! If you'd rather skip some of the schooling and get down to work, here are some books you need to consult.

Abrams, Kathleen, S. *Guide to Careers Without College.* Danbury, Conn.: Franklin Watts, 1995.

Beckett, Kathleen. *Careers Without College: Fashion.* Princeton, N.J.: Peterson's, 1992.

Corwen, Leonard. *College Not Required!: 100 Great Careers That Don't Require a College Degree.* New York: Macmillan, 1995.

Farr, J. Michael. *America's Top Jobs for People Without College Degrees.* Indianapolis: JIST, 1997.

Greenwald, Ted. *Careers Without College: Music.* Princeton, N.J.: Peterson's, 1992.

Peterson, Linda. *Careers Without College: Entertainment.* Princeton, N.J.: Peterson's, 1994.

Unger, Harlow G. *But What If I Don't Want to Go to College?: A Guide to Success through Alternative Education.* Rev ed. New York: Facts On File, 1998.

INDEX

Page numbers in **boldface** indicate main articles. Page numbers in *italics* indicate photographs.